IDENTITY AND EDUCATION: THE LINKS FOR MATURE WOMEN STUDENTS

Identity and Education: The Links for Mature Women Students

JANET PARR
The University of Sheffield, UK

Ashgate

Aldershot • Burlington USA • Singapore • Sydney

Published by
Ashgate Publishing Limited
Gower House
Croft Road
Aldershot
Hampshire GU11 3HR
England

Ashgate Publishing Company
131 Main Street
Burlington
Vermont 05401
USA

Ashgate website: http://www.ashgate.com

British Library Cataloguing in Publication Data
Parr, Janet
 Identity and education : the links for mature women
 students
 1. Women in education - Great Britain 2. Women - Education
 (Higher) - Great Britain - Psychological aspects 3. Women -
 Education (Higher) - Social aspects - Great Britain
 I. Title
 378.1'9822'0941

Library of Congress Catalog Card Number: 99-76658

ISBN 1 84014 997 3

Printed and bound by Athenaeum Press, Ltd.,
Gateshead, Tyne & Wear.

Contents

Preface

Currently, I am a lecturer in the Division of Continuing Education at the University of Sheffield – the same University at which I studied for my BA(Hons) in Sociology and Social Policy. I subsequently taught in further education, before returning to the University part-time to complete my Master of Education, whilst working part-time in higher education. I then once again became a full-time student as well as a part-time lecturer to complete my Ph.D. This route is one well travelled by many lecturers, but very few travel the route as mature women students from working class backgrounds, as I did, when at 36, I became an undergraduate at Sheffield, with a husband and three children to care for and a home to run.

My experiences as a mature student, and those of other mature students whom I have taught, motivated my research which originally set out to look at the barriers which mature women face when they return to learning. What came out from the research was certainly not what I expected. It is difficult to find a single word to describe my feelings of what emerged – the painful, traumatic and compelling narratives of many of the women astounded and angered me, but also filled me with admiration and respect for the ways in which they have coped and are working to change their lives. Their experiences have inspired this book – their accounts are important to be told, and will, I hope, be an inspiration not only to other women following a similar route, but also to the many women whose difficulties are so great that they do not even manage to return to the foot of the educational ladder.

Locating myself in the research

I have spent more than five years researching and working with this powerful material, and have been drawn into the lives of the women through their narratives. I could relate to them, as a woman, as a mature student and as a female from a working class background, now in a respected middle class occupation. Much of what they told me touched my own memories and sparked off such emotions that it is impossible for me to be neutral. Nevertheless, in my selection of the material, which is mostly verbatim

vii

from the women themselves, I have been as conscientious as possible in ensuring an accurate representation of what the women told me. As a feminist writer, it is my belief that values should be transparent, and I think it is important therefore that the reader has a brief overview of my background, which has not only influenced my beliefs but also contributed substantially to the motivation for this research.

A working class background

Born and raised in a mining community, my own mainstream education was limited to just beyond the minimum school leaving age, despite attending a grammar school and gaining eight O-levels. For most of my friends at school, university or college was an automatic next step but there is no memory of this being a topic of conversation with my parents until I reached sixteen when the issue was raised and it was made very clear to me that I was expected to leave school, get a job and contribute to the family income until such time as I married and set up a home of my own. I was however, allowed to remain at school for a year providing I did a secretarial/accounts course which 'will always come in useful'.

This was perhaps not surprising, since no-one in my immediate or extended family had had experience of higher education. Only one person, my aunt had gone to grammar school, and she had left at the minimum leaving age and had gone into domestic service as a maid, following my mother. The patriarchal culture was powerful and the gendered division of labour clear. The women in my immediate and my extended family either did not work or worked in manual or domestic occupations; the married ones fitting any work around the needs and shift-work of the husband and any adult working sons. There was a clear and rigid division of labour - the women did all the domestic chores and childcare, often helping one another out, especially in times of illness. Mealtimes and household jobs were geared around the husband's shift work, mostly at one of the local pits.

The infant school I attended was just down the road and was very much a neighbourhood school, attended by the majority of the local children. Because of the tied nature of the housing, there was at least one miner in each household in the village and all my friends' fathers 'worked at t'pit'. So the whole of my early socialisation was very much influenced by one particular setting, and when as an adult student I read the Dennis, Henriques and Slaughter study 'Coal is our Life' (1956), it was much like reading my own history.

Immediate family influences

Although my step-father had a routine clerical job he was also from a background of manual occupations where there existed a clear gendered division of labour within the home. He had had first-hand experience of the poverty created by the economic depression and the unemployment of the mid 1930s in Liverpool where he was born and raised. From this background, any job was important and a good clerical job was better than a factory job and infinitely better than unemployment. In addition to this, my mother, as well as being an amputee which hampered her mobility, was prone to bouts of illness during the winter, and from the age of 11, I had been running the household from time to time, doing the normal domestic chores which my mother would have done, sometimes being kept home from school. Although I can remember feeling somewhat resentful of this, I never really questioned it - I had been raised in a culture where domestic chores were 'women's work'.

So, on leaving school, a number of secretarial jobs ensued both before and after my marriage at the age of twenty, none of them holding my interest for more than a few months. On getting married, I expected to do, and did, what was normal in my experience - work until children arrived, then stay at home as a full-time housewife. However, a year after the birth of my first child, I was frustrated at home and returned to work part-time, with child-care provided by family and friends, but two more children limited work opportunities outside the home. Although I always managed to earn money in some way, it was generally on a part-time or casual basis and I can clearly remember a feeling of restlessness and a need to do something other than what I was doing, though I never really thought this through.

Returning to education

A casual discussion with a graduate friend I had made whilst running a play group led to my enrolment for an evening class in Sociology at the local college, though I was by no means clear what the subject was about! In hindsight, it is reasonable to say that I was looking for something in my life which wasn't there, but I wasn't sure what it was. I certainly had no long-term goals or 'grand plan' at this stage and had no intention of taking any examinations. The lecturer for Sociology became a firm friend and certainly a 'significant other' in my life, giving me considerable encouragement and support and eventually persuading me to take the A-level examination, enrol for further A-levels the following year and apply to university. This I did, though with some misgivings about my capabilities and the effect on my home life.

When offered a place at university, my feelings were ambivalent - a mixture of pleasure, pride, uncertainty and apprehension; sentiments which have been echoed time and time again by other women students I have met. My insecurity about going to university stayed with me for some time and I can remember applying for routine white collar jobs right up to actually becoming an undergraduate. Quite what I would have done if I had been offered any of these I am not sure!

A mature undergraduate

A grant gave me some independence of income, and I felt that at least my studying was not a burden on the family budget, though this had never been a problem with my husband. However, loneliness was a problem and I was not prepared for the isolation I felt in my first year at university. At 36, I was twice the age of most of the other students, or so I thought, and although there were students who appeared to be nearer my own age, none appeared to be doing the same combination of subjects. In addition, for the majority of the students a university education appeared to have been expected; they appeared to be at home in the system and this made me very aware of the lack of the appropriate 'cultural capital' (Scott, 1991) in my own childhood. My feeling of inferiority, despite having 3 good A-levels, persisted well into the second year, when I discovered that this lack of confidence is quite a common phenomenon among females, regardless of age.

I chose to major in Sociology because the time-table suited my family commitments and daily travelling, although by this time I had more than a passing interest in Psychology. Again, this influence on my choice is something about which many other women mature students have spoken.

Throughout all of my time in further education and university, I had 100 percent support from my husband, who took on many of the roles which had automatically been mine prior to this time, for example giving the children their tea when I was not able to, either because I was late from university or working at home; bathing them; reading the story and putting them to bed. He and the children grew much closer together, and enjoyed this time on their own, but I felt that my husband was doing a job which I should have been doing and my guilt feelings never really disappeared.

My goals whilst at university were fairly short-term - to get through the course and get my degree and I gave little, if any, thought to a future career. My intention had been to take a year out to spend time doing things with my family for which I had had no time over the previous three years, but a chance meeting with a department head at the college where I had done my A-levels, led to the start of my career as a lecturer in further education.

A role model

When I began lecturing, the work was, in large part, with mature women students who often talked, mostly informally, about their reasons for returning to learning, the practicalities of juggling home and education, and their fears of 'not being good enough' for higher education. I talked of my own experiences as a mature student, and many saw me as a role model – I had done it, as an adult with family responsibilities, who was now in a respected profession. Many of these students, like myself, were encouraged to go on from further to higher education and on becoming a university lecturer, I continued with this informal support system, remembering the isolation I had felt during the first year as an adult learner studying at this level.

My interest in the experiences of mature women students subsequently led to in-depth research and I am sure that my own experiences gave me an empathy with the women with whom I have spoken and enabled the traumatic and painful stories which the women talked of to emerge and be told.

Acknowledgements

Without the interest, time, help and support of a great many people, this book would have been impossible.

My sincere thanks go to my supervisor, friend and colleague, David Phillips, who has given his time, energy and patience unstintingly. He has been a tower of strength throughout the whole project.

My grateful thanks also to Ray Thompson, who has meticulously read, re-read and commented on many sections and drafts at various stages.

Sue Boldock and Judy Jackson have done sterling work in transcribing the interview tapes, and Marg Walker did an excellent job of co-ordinating the operation and sorting out the complicated computer transfers.

I would also like to thank the staff of the colleges who found time to talk to me and who gave me every assistance in accessing their teaching groups.

Of course, I owe my greatest debt of thanks to the women who gave their valuable time to talk with me and allowed me to use their stories. Without their help and co-operation, the research would not have been done, nor the book written. I hope that I have presented an honest account of their experiences.

1 Introduction

Why do mature women return to education? On the face of it, the obvious answer is that they wish to gain qualifications which they had not gained at the conventional age. My research indicates though that this is far too simplistic an explanation. For the mature students with whom I spoke (to whom I refer throughout as 'the students' or 'the women'), returning to education seemed to be as much about their identity as it was about paper qualifications. It could almost be described as a 'life-raft' for some students - as one of them said 'it's saved my sanity'. What emerged very clearly from what they said, was the desire to redefine at least part of their identity, to see themselves in a different way and exert a degree of control over some aspects of their lives.

This was so for all the students, but was particularly the case for a number who talked of trauma in their lives, both past and present. Around half of them told me of psychological, physical and sexual abuse, overbearing parents, alcoholism, and the death of a child or other family members. For example, Gerry talked of sexual abuse by her brother at an early age; Jenny spoke of her teenage pregnancy, subsequent marriage to a physically and psychologically abusive partner, as well as of her fight against the cultural restraints of her neighbourhood. Alison talked of a controlling and manipulative father, whereas for Dilys, it was her mother who was the problem. Petra's alcoholic mother meant that she had to take early domestic responsibilities and also care for her sister, whilst she herself was still a child. Della's story, in the concluding chapter, is one of extreme physical and psychological abuse and painful divorce. These experiences were not what I had expected to hear, and certainly not what I had intended to write about, but their awfulness and frequency had such an impact on me that I had no choice but to recount them; to talk of their effect on the women's lives and the links which were made with education.

My original intention, at the outset of the research, had been to investigate the barriers faced by mature women returning to education. My own career as a mature student with family responsibilities and my subsequent lecturing post with adults in both further and higher education,

1

indicated that women, in particular, face a number of specific problems when they return to learning. Some research has been conducted on adult returners, and has tended (though not exclusively) to be quantitative rather than qualitative. This has tended to focus on adults generally, rather than women specifically,[1] although more recent qualitative work which has centred upon adult women as students is emerging to fill this gap in the body of research which exists within this area.[2] My particular interest was in listening to what the women themselves had to say about their return to learning, and with this in mind, I approached a number of educational institutions in my local area.

The Student Group

The forty-nine mature women students who talked with me were attending college or university in or around a northern city which I have called Austen. The city has two universities and a number of colleges of further education. The college sites are located in a variety of geographical and social areas in the city, which range from a deprived area in receipt of European Social Funding, to a clearly affluent area with very different incomes and lifestyles. A range of courses were provided for mature returners which I anticipated would give me a good cross-section of students of different ages, studying different topics. In addition, I spoke with students from a college outside of the city boundaries, since this would draw in students for whom travel and time constraints might be more of an issue than for those students living in or close to the city. This college has just one main site but draws students from an equally wide social distribution.

For the purposes of this research, I defined mature as being 21 or over at the start of the course, since this is the age used by the institutions in my sample. Research by Bell, Hamilton and Roderick (1986) though, does reveal that there is a spread of minimum age for mature student classification across the ages of 21, 23 and 25 depending on the institution or organisation (see also Parr, 1991). However, it is not age so much as the length of time out of the education system before returning which I feel is important, and using 21 as the defining factor was likely to ensure that the woman had had at least three years and probably five or six years out of education before returning.

The majority of the students were on full-time courses. Eight students defined themselves as part-time, though definitions of part-time do vary between educational institutions and between those institutions and various state offices which deal with cash benefits. This is connected with responsibility for course fees. Generally speaking, full-time is defined by the colleges as sixteen hours or more of attendance per week, whereas some students were defining this as part-time. This was particularly relevant to the women's motor vehicle course, which was concentrated into three days of attendance.

The ages of the students ranged from 22 to 50 years, with the majority of women being over 30, and generally partnered. Most had domestic and caring responsibilities which covered both children and elderly dependents. They came from a diverse social demographic background, although it must be pointed out here that my interpretation of the socio-economic group and life-styles of the women is both speculative and subjective, based on geographical location, as I have already indicated, and on what the women told me. My interest was in the women's experiences as women so the research and analysis was based on gender rather than on material circumstances.

The courses

The students were enrolled on a wide range of generally mixed gender courses, both practical and academic which ranged from introductory courses in neighbourhood centres, to degree courses at university. Some of the courses attracted funding from a variety of sources. These were largely those in designated deprived areas, and also those specifically aimed at encouraging women into non-traditional areas, both of which were funded by the European Social Fund. The women on these latter courses were in receipt of an allowance and had access to free crèche facilities. Students on the foundation year of the degree courses were eligible to apply for a mandatory grant. The Access courses were defined by the colleges as full time, so tuition was free, although students did not receive a grant. Senior staff at all the college sites were helpful in discussing with me the provision which was made for mature students in general, and women in particular, as well as the courses which would give a range of women to talk with.

The interviews

The women were in no way 'selected' for interview, the only criterion being that they should be over 21, and were randomly drawn from those in the various groups I spoke to, who volunteered to meet and talk with me. The students interviewed on the different courses largely reflect the numbers of students enrolled on those courses, though the sample is by no means mathematically proportionate (see Parr, 1996 for further details). All of them were white, since no black students came forward for interview. I had given considerable thought to the sampling procedure, and felt that to try and combine factors such as age, partnered status, caring responsibilities and so on with the different types of courses would be problematic, especially for those courses with small numbers.

This style is also very much in line with the grounded theory[3] approach I was taking, which involves a constant interaction, right from the start, between all the research processes - data collection, analysis beginning soon after with ongoing review of the collection process, the development of conceptual frameworks and theories from the data, and the testing of ideas.

I met and talked with the women in a variety of settings, including the colleges and universities, their homes, and even on three occasions, in my car. All the interviews except one were taped, with the agreement of the students, and transcribed, since I felt that this was far less intrusive than scrambling notes down, whilst at the same time trying to watch body language and think about what the woman was saying.

My desire to hear the women's stories led me towards an appreciative ethnographic research style (for further details, see Parr, 1996). This qualitative approach highlighted what had been a major issue in my mind and which I felt would be emphasised with the relative intimacy of a loosely structured interview situation, where I had a great deal in common with the women with whom I was talking. I aimed to create an easy, comfortable interactive situation in which the women could ask questions of me if they so wished. I wanted to answer these questions as honestly as possible without driving the interview down a particular route. My own values had clearly informed the research but I did not want them to unduly influence the women's stories. My interest in this area stems from my own experiences as a mature student and as a lecturer in further education working mostly with adults, and I was aware that my background and experiences could both facilitate and hinder the data collecting and analysis. I also recognised that my own internalised concepts could limit my perception and thus my ability to be open and receptive to new ideas and concepts emerging from the data. It is impossible of course to ignore one's own values as I have said in the Preface, and in fact all recent feminist methodology emphasises that it is important for the researcher to locate herself in the research and acknowledge the inherent bias, which can be viewed as being positive as well as negative.

Selection of the material I have presented, from the wealth I was given, has clearly been mine and designed to illustrate the links between identity and education. However, my aim has been to enable the women's voices to be heard, although in order to protect them, the women's names and the names of the institutions they were attending have been changed. My desire to represent them accurately means that it is mostly their narratives which are used in the book and I have generally reproduced their words verbatim. Although I have occasionally paraphrased and edited what they told me, this has been limited. As Reissman says:

> Speech that has been 'cleaned up' to be more readable loses important information. (Reissman, 1987, p.189)

A strength of the grounded theory approach I took is an emphasis on open-mindedness, a willingness to listen, hear and act on the results at all times. I took every precaution not to drive the interviews down the route of 'barriers' which had been my original topic, and to some extent was vindicated by the emergence of the unsolicited and unexpected data, which forms the focus of this book.

This relaxed approach created an atmosphere in which the women felt free to talk openly. This is evident in **chapter two**, which begins by discussing the reasons which the students initially gave, at the start of the interview, for returning to education. They talked of factors such as a better job, better qualifications, contributing to the family income, a testing of ability and a realisation of their potential in comparison with significant others. There was however a major shift in their explanations and later in the interview they talked of status, proof of ability, a public as well as a private identity and a general need to 'do something for myself'.

Some of the women had begun to compare their ability with others who were better qualified and were beginning to question the way in which their own ability had been defined. A number of students verbalised a long-held desire to return to education and often used opportunities like redundancy to fulfil this ambition. For others, the return to education was rather tentative and was really a trying out of their ability to cope with academic work. Finally, for a number of women, there was a therapeutic component to their return to education. The chapter ends with a discussion of these changing reasons, links them with a desire for women to change their lives, and talks of the social pressures on women to conform to a particular identity.

The concept of identity is pivotal to the women's stories, and is closely inter-linked with power and control. **Chapter three** discusses the social influences on our identity and the links between these influences and the women's return to education. Clearly, there is no single characteristic which makes up our identity, but a multiplicity of elements which may be divided broadly into biological and social influences.

The students I talked with have a biological identity as women, but their roles as daughter, mother and wife are affected by the cultural norms of this society and are thus part of their social identity. In a predominantly patriarchal culture, the identities of both women and men will be influenced by a male-powerful ideology. Walby's (1990) six patriarchal structures of household, work, male violence, sexuality, culture and the state are used as a framework for discussion of influences on identity and verbatim material from the students is incorporated in illustration.

The links between identity and education were made in a variety of ways: proof of ability, a better job; sometimes simply associated with the status which education was perceived as bringing with it. Particularly for those who were partnered and/or had domestic responsibilities, links were often made between education and their domestic identity. This was particularly powerful with one student, Colette:

> I wanted to do something for myself, yes for myself. I didn't want to
> be a mum with two kids. I wanted to do something for myself and
> not she's somebody's mum and that's Paul's wife type of thing ...

Colette goes on to talk more about this and the chapter then links her with other students who told me of extremely painful life experiences and will draw out, in a very general way, the links between these stories and education, as an introduction to the following four chapters.

The shift from barriers to trauma

Right from the start of the interviews, unexpected and unsolicited findings were emerging. All the hurdles which I had expected the women to have to negotiate in their return to education were there. In addition to this though, the students were talking to me about personal issues in their lives, including painful experiences. Because I was focusing on barriers, I did not at first see the importance of these experiences, but I felt that if the women had been prepared to give precious time in a busy schedule to talk to me, the least I could do was to listen to what they wanted to tell me - in ethical terms, a 'win-win' situation. I noted these stories with interest though and can remember commenting to my colleagues on the trauma in some of the women's backgrounds.

I used the word 'trauma' because of the powerful and painful nature of what the women were telling me. These experiences had clearly had a major impact on the lives of the students, and the effects appeared to be ongoing. As I interviewed more students, I began to realise that they were emerging frequently, and seemed to be as much the rule as the exception. I did consider though whether the impact of what the women were saying was staying with me and colouring my thinking. By this time I had completed about fifteen interviews I realised that a large proportion of the women with whom I spoke were talking of painful experiences in their past. I was stunned at the frequency of these stories, and as they emerged, I mentally fitted them into my original framework of barriers - these painful experiences were major hurdles which the women had surmounted, or were surmounting, in their return to education.

By the time the interviews had been completed, around half of the forty nine women had told me of painful life experiences which could be significantly linked with their return to learning as adults. I was surprised at the way these experiences tumbled out with no prompting and I was appalled at their frequency. It was at this point that I decided that these stories and their links with education should be told.

The problem of definition

Initially, I used the word trauma to describe these experiences, since they appear to have had a considerable negative effect on the women, but felt very uncomfortable with the word, since for me it implied almost a 'one-off' occurrence, which in some cases is true, but in others, the women are coping with ongoing painful experiences. I spent more than a year trying to think of an alternative word or phrase to adequately describe what the women told me. I have been offered phrases such as 'post-traumatic syndrome' and 'significantly meaningful events', neither of which seemed to portray what the women were telling me. I re-focused my thinking and concentrated on the content of the women's narratives. The problem has been to find terminology to adequately reflect the range of ordeals about which the women spoke. I considered again my initial use of the word trauma to describe the women's experiences. A good dictionary suggests shock, ordeal or crisis as synonymous with trauma, and some recent reading in psychology defined trauma as the creation of psychological damage which can have lasting effects on lives and may engender a feeling of helplessness, creating an emotional wound. This much wider concept of the word does represent the broad range of the women's stories, so I have come full circle, but rather than simply using the word 'trauma' I will also use the phrase 'traumatic experiences' to describe what the women told me, since for a number of them these experiences have been ongoing throughout their lives.

Traumatic experiences

During the initial analysis of the data, I found it very hard to get away from the impact of the women's experiences. Each was unique, had clearly been painful, and had a major effect on the women's lives. I was pulled into the content of the stories, as a woman, as someone who had also been through some of what they were telling me and also as a past mature student whose return to education was for many reasons other than education itself. I was both angry and hurt for the women and it was difficult to see beyond this to any patterns or groupings in the data. Empathy, I have discovered, is a double-edged sword, both enabling and disabling. I read and re-read the transcripts and made summaries and notes until the anger and pain began to subside and I began to see some patterns emerging. Analysis of qualitative material is of course often fraught with this type of difficulty, and particularly so with emotive material.[3] I made many different attempts at grouping such as using the age of the student; the age at which the experiences occurred; the experiences themselves; the intensity of the experience; the partnered and domestic status of the woman. Although all were important, it was clear from the data that discrete categories were going to be difficult for much of the material. I finally settled on two broad categories, though as the reader will recognise, there is considerable overlap and interweaving.

The first category is concerned with the impact of major life events or changes, and they are discussed in **chapter four**. These events may have affected the student directly – divorce, serious injury or illness and redundancy are mentioned. For example, until her return to education, Liz could only see in her future the possibility of being wheelchair bound when a serious back injury forced her to give up her nursing career. Students were also affected indirectly, as with Heather, whose parents' death, both within a year, made her look at her own life and needs. Whatever form the event or change took, it appears to have made the woman re-assess her life and what she wanted from it.

The second category is concerned with what I have called restrictive stultifying experiences - traumatic episodes with lasting and damaging psychological effects. This latter category is divided into three sub-groups: in the first group, which is the focus of **chapter five**, the women talked of painful experiences in their childhood. Although most of the experiences about which the women spoke had some roots in what happened in their childhood years, some women actually focused upon their childhood and early teens as having had a major and negative effect on their lives. For Alison and Dilys, it was a restrictive and controlling parent, but some students also talked of wider social influences on their lives – both Vida and Aurora, for example, experienced cultural racism in their childhood, which they consider had a negative effect on their identity.

The second sub-group is concerned with the effects of unplanned pregnancies and **chapter six** focuses on women whose painful experiences began just out of childhood. It draws out the links between education and identity made by four women who had become pregnant in their teens and entered into restrictive, stultifying and sometimes violent relationships. The return to learning for these students has strong links with confidence, independence and a desire to prove their ability.

To the third sub-group, in **chapter seven**, I have given the title 'mega-trauma' because of the nature and ongoing effects of what the women have lived through, and in some cases are still living through. The students talked of trauma which began early in their childhood and have continued, perhaps in different forms, into and through their adulthood. Psychological trauma, physical abuse, and sometimes both, separate these students out from the others in the seemingly continuous effects of their painful experiences. Again, though the women's histories are individual, they are connected through their talk of the effects of education on their confidence, self-image and independence.

Categorisation in this manner is clearly not the only way of organising the material and a re-working of the data may well produce different structures. What is important to remember though is that the structure I have used has been drawn from what the women have said; how they perceive and describe their experiences, and the links they make between these experiences and education.

The **concluding chapter** draws the threads of the women's stories together and its central theme is the links which the women are making with education now. It is very clear that the students were gaining a great deal more from their return to education than just paper qualifications. A number of common strands emerged and students talked either directly or indirectly about issues of power and control, independence, ability, a better self-image, self-perception, confidence and fulfilment, status, a public as well as a private identity and the need to 'do something for myself', as the following examples from some of the students indicate:

> It's made me value me a lot I think, it's made me see myself a lot
> differently, and I'm a lot happier about myself.
> It boosts your confidence and it all makes you feel much better.
>
> It's something to be proud of - something for yourself ...

I might not get chance to do much with it but at least I know I've achieved something ...

I need that identity and independence.

It just goes back to saying I want to be independent. I must say that independence is very strong, but also an identity is very very important.

Indeed, confidence and fulfilment are common threads connecting all the students, but they are perhaps more powerfully evident in those women who talked of painful life experiences. In the final part of this chapter Della's account of psychological and physical abuse epitomises how the women are rejecting some of the ways in which they have been defined and have taken some control over re-shaping their identity to present a more acceptable image for themselves and for others.

Notes

1. See for example, Wakeford, 1993; FEU, 1991; Pye, 1991; Browning, 1990; Hughes et al, 1989; Woodley et al, 1987; Schutze et al, 1987; Charnley et al, 1985; Lucas and Ward, 1985; ACACE, 1982.
2. Parr, 1996, 1991; Coats, 1994, 1989; Pascall and Cox, 1993; McGivney, 1993; Edwards, 1993.
3. Glazer and Strauss, 1967; Strauss and Corbin, 1990; Taylor and Bogdan, 1984; Miles and Huberman, 1994.

2 Why do women return to education?

One of my opening questions, almost as an 'icebreaker' at the start of the interview was to ask the women why they had returned to learning as adults. The initial replies gave quite practical reasons such as wanting to contribute to the family income, better qualifications and a more stimulating job. Women with children told me that it was virtually impossible to get a job which fitted in with school hours, or which paid enough for childcare, and were taking the opportunity to gain a better education whilst their children were small. However, when I revisited the question of why they had returned to education, later in the interview, I was given much more personal reasons and the women spoke of status, esteem, and a need to prove ability, and for some women, there was a therapeutic component to their studying. These practical and personal reasons are not mutually exclusive, and the chapter concludes with a discussion of this.

Many students talked about a rejection of mainstream schooling, a realisation of under achievement in their compulsory education and wanting more from their lives than they were getting. Some of the women had begun to compare their ability with others who were better qualified and were beginning to question the way in which their own ability had been defined. A number of students verbalised a long-held desire to return to education and a few had used opportunities like redundancy to fulfil this ambition. For others though, the return to education was rather tentative and was really a trying out of their ability to cope with academic work.

The chapter begins by outlining some of the original reasons before moving on to look at how the women modified and expanded their responses. Early in the interviews, Heather, Colette and Gloria talked about finance.

Helping with family finances

The students in this situation told me that it was virtually impossible to get a job which either fitted in with school hours or paid enough to enable them to purchase child-care. Many linked their return to education with the family budget. They mentioned that better qualifications would give them a better paid job and they would be better able to contribute to the family income when the children were older. Some women had actually opted for a particular course because it provided a grant.

Heather is 39, married with three young children and is enrolled on a funded women's course. This is a full-time course which attracts EEC funding because it provides non-traditional training for women. It is free, pays a small allowance and provides free crèche facilities:

> Heather: The main thing, like, I've got three young children and ... a second income's always 'andy so we (she and other students) were looking for something that paid an allowance as well as ... you know ... coming back into college ...

Colette is 31, married with two children aged 4 and 6. She is enrolled on the same course as Heather:

> Colette: I think basically it was so that I could get a job, you know once I got the kids off my hands ... Really it does boil down to your money situation as well doesn't it? I mean the life we live today is very money oriented and you do struggle on one wage with two small children - you want to do things you can't.

Gloria, who is 38, married with two children aged 11 and 9, is a student on the foundation year of a four-year degree in science. Gloria's economic reason had a slightly different angle:

> Gloria: If I can get a decent job at the end of this then Jim can go off and fly Kilimanjaro or something like that - which is what he wants to do. So I will be the provider then ...

Linked to their wish to contribute to the family income, these students had a general desire to gain better qualifications. Annabel's aim was much more specific. She had been working for some time as a motor mechanic and wanted the paper qualifications associated with her practical skills.

Better qualifications

Annabel is 30, single with no children. She is studying part-time in her second year to gain her NVQ in Motor Mechanics:

> Annabel: I need the qualification really ... I did think I'd learn something as well. Now I'm just here for the qualification. I wanted the practical and the learning, so I have more confidence to go out for jobs.

Like Annabel, many women, at least initially in the interview, linked their return to education with better qualifications and ultimately what they felt would be a better job. This was regardless of whether the women had recently been in the job market or had been out of it for some time.

A more stimulating job

For instance, in order to study again, some women had actually given up a job which they found unfulfilling. Faith and Sam are two examples of this.

Faith, who is 32 and married with a child, is a student enrolled on a social science access course at a local college, after which she is hoping to go to university. She gave up her well-paid job as an air stewardess with a major airline in order to return to study on a social science access course:

> Faith: I used to be an air stewardess ... for five years - long haul. A brilliant job, well paid, went everywhere in the world but, you know, not very mind stimulating. I think you get to a stage in your life ... I didn't want to be a sixty year old stewardess because, you know, you can work up until you're about sixty, but I'd always wanted to educate myself but never really thought about it, and I don't know, it was like a turning point in my life really.
>
> The job I was doing wasn't stimulating my mind and I think, when you get a bit older your child makes you realise, you know, what can you offer your child? And I thought, 'I'm either going to have to work like on a counter, like in Woolworth's, to give him money' - because I couldn't foresee me doing that job for a long time you see. And I thought, 'well no because I want to do a better job' and the only way to get a better job is to educate myself really. So - I want to be a psychologist!

Sam is 26 and living with her partner in a stable relationship. She gave up her job as a medical secretary to study on the foundation year of a four-year science degree:

> Sam: I'd worked as a medical secretary for 6 years and I was getting a bit frustrated with my job, lots of changes happening within the Health Service and in the department I worked in and I was getting just more and more fed up doing the same thing and not being sort of appreciated for what you do, and not thought of as having the brain power ... I really enjoyed the job for about the first four years but then I sort of became unsettled and thought well, I can cope with a bit more than this, looking round at women I was working with who were sort of 40 and still having to run round after all these people and

I was thinking 'oh I don't want to be doing that, I want to have a bit more say, have a bit more out of my job when I get to their age'.

Both Faith and Sam were well trained for the job which they were doing and had skills which were transferable into similar occupations. However, both felt that once acquired, this skill took little mental effort to apply and their return to education was aimed at gaining better qualifications and an occupation which taxed their mental capacities more.

Ursula is 32, single with no dependants. She is enrolled on the first year of a science foundation course which is franchised out from one of the local universities. She left school and trained as a nurse, but could only get night work when she finished her training, so she left after 8 months. She returned to college and trained as a medical secretary, but hated the sexist and superior attitude of the doctors and again left. Her last occupation was with a travel/time-share company, from which she was made redundant, but again she mentioned the sexist and superior attitudes of male staff towards secretaries. I asked her what she disliked about being a secretary:

> Ursula: Oh people treat you horrible. Shocking. They treat you like that as a nurse as well. You're a paid slave. People think that just because you're a nurse, you can make them cups of tea and wait on them ... Terrible. And then you get all this between doctors and nurses - the doctors treat you very badly ... they treat you like an inferior.

> Men have a funny attitude towards secretaries I find. I think perhaps they use it to make themselves look better in a way. 'cos a boss and a secretary relationship's a bit like a husband and wife sort of thing. And they treat you very much in the same vein, don't they? But they do have a very subservient attitude and I hated it. I couldn't stand it. I hated somebody treating me like some glossy little doll. So that's why I got out of that one - basically. I wouldn't do it again.

Ursula links her return to learning with her rejection of the school ethos in her mainstream education, which was echoed by other students.

Rejection of school ethos

Many students talked about a realisation of having 'wasted' their opportunities in mainstream education, though for different reasons:

Ursula appeared to have had better educational opportunities in her youth than the average child, but her obvious dislike of the school was threaded through the whole interview. She associates her lack of achievement and fulfilment with her early school experiences.

Ursula: I just messed about at school. And I didn't work hard enough. I went to a dreadful school which I hated. It was an all girls school and I couldn't stand it.

I started at eleven 'cos you have to take an entrance exam - it was one of these Girls Public Day School Trust schools. So you had to take this entrance exam and I took the entrance exam and went there because my elder sister went there as well. I was just in the wrong environment. It was all very disciplined, it was all very, kind of, 'Miss Jean Brodie' style and I just hated it.

I did O levels and stayed on to do my A levels but I failed them because I messed about and didn't do anything. I just hated the school and I wanted to get out. My approach to things was totally different. I just wanted to get a job. So I applied to do nursing. My dad was a doctor as well, so it was, kind of a medicine type thing.

I think my basic school education was a lot of the problem of why I didn't go to university when I was younger. I think that's had quite a lasting effect on my education.

I just think it's a false environment to bring children up in. You either get totally insular or you become a rebel, and I rebelled. I wasn't on drugs or anything ... I suppose I rebelled against the system in a lot of ways, yes. I can't tell you how much I hated it. I mean, I just didn't do any work because I didn't like it and - it was dreadful. I think that was it, you know. I think it does have a lot to do with why you don't go (to university).

Go and have a look at this school and you'll see! Go in there and talk to them and the people and see what they say.

Faith left school at the minimum leaving age, rejecting academic education and trained to be a model, before working as an air stewardess:

Faith: I did quite well at school, I got six O levels and then my Dad wanted me to go to college. My dad always said education is the keyword. And I thought, 'Oh no, I'll be a model'. So I just ignored it completely and went off and did all the glamorous things I'd always wanted to do.

I actually tried to go college just as I was doing my modelling, and I think that was more because I thought I'd be a student and a model 'cos it sounded good - not because I actually really wanted to go back to college. And I actually remember sitting in a Sociology class when I was about eighteen and I just thought, 'This is such a load of bollocks. I can't believe how pathetic this class is'. Now I'm doing exactly the same thing now that I was then, but I find it so interesting. I think it was just that then I wasn't interested and I didn't have a thirst for learning and education. But I do realise now and I just think it's so important. It's changed me completely.

Denise, who is 42 and a divorced mother of three, is in her second year of a social science access course. She felt cheated by having 'failed' the 11+ and gone to a secondary modern school:

Denise: I felt very cheated by that. I hadn't got the qualifications or any sort of education. I went to a secondary modern school in Cambridge and when I look back on it, I was far brighter than the kids around me and I was bored. I rebelled. I didn't work at school and I put my energy into creating disturbances. In the guide company, I was mixing with all these grammar school girls and holding my own confidently. I think that fed my anger and my feeling of disappointment and rebellion that the system was crap ...

Not all students made such clear links between their early educational experiences and their return to learning. For many women, there was a growing realisation that their potential was unfulfilled. Here, the women are beginning to express more personal reasons for returning to formal study, as well as the more practical ones which they advanced.

More personal reasons for returning

When I revisited the question 'why have you come back into education?' part-way through the interview, I found that whereas the majority of women made links with employment initially, most subsequently told me that they were doing it for themselves and mentioned a variety of reasons. Some of these reasons were clearly connected with employment, such as the status which a degree would bestow, but there were other, more personal reasons such as confidence, proof of ability, therapy, and a public as well as a private identity.

Confidence and status

Nola who is 36, married with two children is enrolled on a social science access course at a local college. She told me initially that she was aiming for a degree because she did not want to go back into the same clerical work, but lower down the scale, which she felt was inevitable, having been out of the job market for a few years. However, she went on, later in the interview to talk about confidence, and the esteem which she felt a degree would give her:

> I left school early, and I have not got any qualifications, and I think you lose an awful lot of confidence as well, especially with not working. This is a challenge for me. This is a hurdle I have got to get over. It's like amateur dramatics, you know, because that's a challenge for me - I had to push myself to say 'You have got to do it, you have just got to walk on stage there and say your lines'. I pushed myself and I did it. That's what this is as well, I just view it as a challenge. I mean, it all boosts your confidence and it all makes you feel much better.
>
> There's another thing why I thought I would like to get a degree, because I always feel that for those people that haven't gone on to higher education, they always have this 'chip on their shoulder' sort of attitude. I just feel that if I do go and I do get a degree, it's like a lot of my friends in Edinburgh, I mean they are solicitors, and I look at them, and we sit and we chat, and I think 'you're no more intelligent than me but because you have got this degree and because of the job that you are doing, people assume that you are'.

Implicit in what Nola says is her need to prove her ability, which was a sentiment verbalised by many of the students, either directly, as a reason for returning, or indirectly, in the expression of both relief and pleasure that their ability was being proved on the course.

Proof of ability

Ursula, Denise and Grace are just three of the students who made clear links with wanting to prove their ability. Ursula's return to education was directly linked with her desire for a more fulfilling job, but she also wants to prove to herself that she has the ability - not to do the academic work which she was quite confident about, but whether she had the stickability:

> Ursula: I wanted to do it for myself as well really. I mean, it wasn't just for a career, to get a better job. I didn't think, 'Oh well I want to earn loads of money so I'll go and get a degree'. I did it a lot for myself really. Just to show myself that I could do it 'cos I knew I could. I knew that academically I've got the capability to do it, I just, sort of questioned whether I'd got the motivation and the commitment really ...

Denise enrolled on an access course as a tentative testing of her ability:

> Denise: I think I came back thinking 'am I bright or am I deceiving myself?' I've always wanted a degree ... it's no good having these aspirations if I can't do the work. I knew I could talk articulately; I knew that I could write articulately, but I didn't know whether I could remember facts ... an access course was a gentle way into education. After the first half year I suppose, I realised that I could do this very easily and it was wonderful to realise that.

I met Denise by chance when she was at university the following year, and whilst saying that she did not like the impersonality of a big institution and missed the small group support she had had at college, she expressed pleasure that she was coping very well with the work.

Grace is 46 and has been divorced for 10 years. For this student, who attends a neighbourhood centre, proving her ability is also linked with proving to her ex-husband that she could survive on her own after her divorce. Her return to education started with basic typing courses, aiming to get a marketable skill, but it seems that her horizons are broadening. Although she talks about getting a job, she has only seriously applied for two, both part-time, at the centre she attends for her classes. She gets much satisfaction from knowing she has some academic ability, and again, confidence is mentioned:

> Grace: I'm divorced and I knew eventually I'd have to get a job and I first started doing a typing course ... I didn't know there were all these different courses then ... Now I know that I've got ability to do things, I'm not an idiot ... I'm not a dumb blonde ... nobody can take off me what I've learnt. Jill (the course tutor) mentioned about university and I thought, 'well, there's another thing to think about'.

> I've found out I can do things that I didn't know I could do before. I think I've got more confidence now than what I've ever had really. My ex-husband said, 'Oh you'll never survive on your own'. I thought, 'well, I'll show him'.

Like Grace, many students made clear links between their past lives, experiences and their return to education. They saw it as an opportunity to change at least a part of their life, whatever their circumstances and to establish a new identity.

Whereas Grace's discovery of her ability began whilst she was in education, for some students it was a degree of self-assessment which motivated their return to learning.

Comparison with significant others

For Denise, Nola and Rhona for example, there had been a growing questioning of their defined ability in relation to others:

> Denise: When my children were little, I got involved with a voluntary organisation and I mixed with educated women and I realised that there was no difference between their intelligence and my intelligence. I realised I could do more than what my education had led me to believe I could do ...

Nola very quickly became bored with each job she had, and then resentful of both pay and status differences between her and the professionals with whom she worked:

> Nola: I just got so bored; it was always, 'I need more than this. I am better than this. I can do better than this'. Then when I got to the solicitors' office and I thought 'I can do this'. I have always had in the back of my mind, if I had the chance, I would like to do a law degree. I've always seen these other people and thought 'I could do that'. Especially in London, my boss used to give me all his jobs and go 'Nola, could you do this, could you do that', and I used to think 'Why are you getting paid all this money, and I am sitting here checking deeds and things for you?'.

Rhona is 49, and enrolled on a full-time humanities access course. She is married and up to the birth of her son, who is now 10, had done secretarial work and became a Personal Assistant which involved much travel and responsibility. She told me she began to think about her own education when she realised that she was confusing intelligence with education:

> Rhona: When I worked with all these graduates, I thought this is brilliant you know, they're so fantastic, they're so educated and they're so clever and I used to think that for a long time. I respected them more because I think I respect people who are intelligent, like my friend Diane. But she's just well educated and that set me thinking about 10 years ago, she's just well educated, and she's no more intelligent than me ...

When the students did return to education, it was often 'water testing' - a tentative exploration of what courses were being offered, and whether they could cope with it academically.

Water testing

Denise is one of those students whose return to education was very tentative. Deidre is 48, divorced and on a full-time funded course, at a local college. After a serious operation, which she talks of later, she knew she wanted to return to learning, but was unsure of courses or her ability:

> Denise: I was just looking round all the time for something that was right for me. So I went on a couple of taster days ... I think I came back wondering 'am I bright, am I deceiving myself', you know? 'Is this a possibility?' I didn't have a plan as such ...

Deidre seems to be testing her ability very tentatively, not wanting to take the next step before she is sure that she can do it.

> Deidre: Well, for long enough now I've wanted to come back into education. I've been unemployed for quite a long time now and I wanted to really know if I could actually do anything academic-wise. I think I'd like to take a subject up that would involve maths and physics. Maths I'm not doing too well in, so I do extra maths, but the physics I'm getting about 60 percent, so I'm not doing too bad there. I can't decide whether I want to go into further, higher education, or just go for employment. It really depends on how well I do on this course. I wanted to know how well I'd done up to Christmas before I applied. From what I can gather, I'm not doing too bad really.

Some students were much less tentative in their approach than this, and many told me that returning to learning had been a long-held ambition.

Fulfilment of a long-held ambition

Both Joy and Olga emphasised this aspect of their studies and had used the opportunity of their redundancy to further their education.

Joy is 38 and partnered with no children. Her redundancy gave her the opportunity to do something which has been at the back of her mind for some time. She was grammar school educated and left with six O-levels, following this with a bi-lingual secretarial course at her local college. Recently, she has generally had administrative posts, but was made redundant. Finance was an issue and she told me that she could probably not have come back into education if she had not been able to get a grant:

> Joy: Well it's been something that I would do one day for years and years and years and I was made redundant at the end of May and I had a couple of friends who had done the access course and I came for an interview and I discovered that it might be possible to get a

grant and it just all fell into place. It was just like something made sense saying this is the way, so that's why it all came together at the right time. I think if I'd not have been made redundant it would still be something that I was thinking I would do later, something to be forced into really ... I had done a whole range of admin. jobs that had been interesting but I realised that I was never going to get any further than I had doing the work that I had been doing. I wanted the interest. I could see that it enriches your life in all sorts of ways and I wanted that.

Olga, who is 40 and has done a variety of jobs, is married with three sons, none of whom are dependent. She has a clear career aim to become a nurse, has enrolled on the science access course at a local college and been offered a place on a nursing degree at a local university. She sees her redundancy as an opportunity which came at the right time for her, since her three children are no longer dependent upon her:

Olga: I was made redundant. I actually worked in adult education for seven years and then, for various reasons, I came out of adult education and went into the building trade, in sales and then as a buyer, and I was made redundant a year last February. I talked to various people who said, 'well, you know, why don't you go for a degree?' I've got a place on a degree course starting in September.

Olga, like Ursula and Denise above, told me that she had been a bit of a rebel at school. All three implied that they were aware of unfulfilled potential, and like most students, were aiming to change their public identity.

A public as well as a private identity

In particular, many women with partners and domestic responsibilities saw education as giving them a public identity separate from the private identity located in their caring and housekeeper role. Moira, Olive and Edna expressed some of the sentiments which were reflected in most of the interviews with this group of students:

Moira, who is 47 and married with two adult sons is enrolled on a social science access course. She gave up her paid employment when she became pregnant and has not worked seriously outside the home for twenty years:

Moira: I suddenly thought, 'Well, I know I'm capable of more than hoovering and cleaning up day after day after day, but I don't know what I'm capable of, so I'll go and try. Just see what is in there, or if there is anything there!' 'Cos you want to just spark it up again if there is anything there. I felt as if there was a little bit of something in there that I wanted to fulfil, but I wasn't sure what it was. I couldn't put my finger on it and say, 'that's what I need', but I knew there was something I needed.

Olive is 31 and married with three children. She is enrolled on the first year of a four year combined studies degree course, franchised out from a local university. Olive, whose interview was noted, not recorded, told me that she was 'screamingly bored' and wanted something other than children to talk about and to. She felt that in the home, she had lost her identity 'I'm Mike's wife, Joe's mum, never me'. She went on to say that she tried not to let college work interfere with her time with the children but that her work was important. She told me that her family recognised the change in her, and 'Joe told me last week that I was a nicer person since I'd been at college' - she felt she was a person 'in my own right'.

Edna is 51, and her husband has had a stroke. She is enrolled on the women's motor vehicle course and told me that her main reason for joining the course was to learn about engines, but this was not the only benefit she gained:

> Edna: I were learning to drive and I wanted to know how the car worked, it's as simple as that! No, actually it's eased the situation at home because I was getting tied up and a bit depressed I suppose - being in the house all the time. Since my husband had this stroke, things just started to build up, you know? I came purposely to learn about the engines and that - but it has eased the situation at home as well. I love getting out of the house. I've met new friends you know, and I'm learning a bit. I like coming and I think, with me coming to college, it gives him that break when the children are at school, for a bit of time on his own. So it gives him that break as well. We're not on top of each other all the time.

> Well I mean, for thirty odd years I've been a housewife and mother and I've never been out of the house ... I enjoy coming out. I mean, I can just come here, do it and go straight back. But I've been out, and I'm enjoying what I'm doing.

Clearly, with Edna, as with many other women, there are a number of benefits from education. She is gaining knowledge of motor vehicles but in addition she is gaining a 'here and now' benefit from education. It is giving her an identity outside the home, and enjoyment in what she is doing. Many other students talked about this, for example, Vida is a 35 year old 2nd year university student, married with three children:

> Vida: This university thing is something for me. It didn't belong to Jeremy and it didn't belong to the kids, it's mine ... Often I would go in early and have a coffee and read my book before I was going to a lecture but as I walk through that door it's like a physical feeling that I had left everything else behind and this was my world ...

Another 'here and now' benefit gained from returning to education was the therapeutic effect for some students and for one of them, this was a direct reason for her return to study.

Therapy

It could be argued that returning to education was therapeutic for many of the students, since this type of benefit can be seen in many of the stories. For some women though, this was mentioned specifically. For Netta and Liz, education as therapy was one of the main reasons for their returning, but for Heather, it was an added bonus. She told me that the course acted as therapy for her after the recent and unexpected death of both her parents:

> I don't know what I would have done if I hadn't got this to look forward to and to occupy me .. I'm really grateful that I'd got it, that I were on the course and that I come on it and just sunk myself into it.

Liz's experiences were more directly personal - she has a severe back problem. Her story is told in the next section, but it is worth noting here what she says about the therapeutic nature of her return to learning:

> Liz: I used to think, 'in a few years you're going to be in a wheelchair', or something like that. I used to dwell on it an awful lot whereas I don't now. It hasn't gone away. That problem hasn't gone away but I can see other things, I can see beyond it.

Netta, who is studying on the same course as Heather, is 23 and married with two children, aged three and four, enrolled on medical advice:

> Netta: My doctor and my health visitor actually told me to come back to college because I was suffering from depression - from being stuck in the house I was told. That's why I went part time last year and it did help, so I came full time this year. I don't have time to be depressed any more - too busy ... I'm finding something else to do with my time and not have to look after the kids all day ...

The therapeutic aspect of Netta's course is linked with her need for an identity outside of the domestic arena, but it also gives her some financial independence because she gets a grant.

> I get £28.00 per week which is standard for everybody. It goes into my own little bank account and I'm taking driving lessons out of it so I can make myself more mobile ...

Netta had enrolled on a non-traditional course for women and was aiming to move into engineering or manufacturing systems at university. Though she had no clear career path, she was adamant that she would not work in traditionally female occupations. Like other students, her reasons for returning to learning were more complex than would appear at first sight.

Contradictory or complementary explanations?

So why would the students apparently alter the reasons they gave me for returning to education? On the whole, I think there is no contradiction between the practical and the personal reasons, rather it is an expansion. Economic reasons and personal reasons are not necessarily mutually exclusive since our status in this society is largely influenced by the type of job we do, but it seems to me that some women initially advanced what could be perceived as a socially acceptable reason for returning to education. In our culture, women are constantly being told, both directly and indirectly to put others' needs before their own. Women are still seen as the primary (and often unpaid) carers - of the young, their partners and the elderly (see amongst many others, Warde and Hetherington, 1993; Charles, 1993; Nash, 1990; Brannen and Moss, 1988) and this is reflected in most institutions of our society and particularly in the benefits system (Lewis, 1991; Maclean and Groves, 1991; Williams, 1989; Rose, 1985; Wilson, 1983). It can also be seen in the types of jobs women do - the majority who work outside the home are employed in the caring or service industries (CSO, Social Trends, 1999). The fact that most married women with dependent children, who work outside the home are employed part-time is a reflection of their domestic and caring responsibilities (CSO, Social Trends, 1999). Even though advertising has changed considerably, women are still represented as taking prime responsibility for family care and domestic chores. For example, in both magazines and television, food and washing powder advertisements have a female in the central role of responsibility, where the implication is that whatever else a woman may do, she is still responsible for the everyday, ongoing caring and household chores. Very few men are shown in this position and where they are, they are often shown as inept. This is of course a representation which both reflects and creates a reality - that at least part of women's identity is located in the domestic and caring role. This seems true even when women are in paid employment and hence we have the 'superwoman syndrome' - participate in the public sphere by all means, but the private sphere is still your responsibility (for a good exposition of this, see Newell, 1993).

It is perhaps not surprising then that for those women with domestic and caring responsibilities, 'doing it for myself' may have been construed by the students as a somewhat selfish reason and the economic reasons which were advanced were more socially acceptable reasons to give to a relative stranger. However, once the women felt more relaxed in the discussion and an element of trust had been created, they felt more able to give me other, not necessarily mutually exclusive, reasons for their return to education. There is also of course the possibility that in thinking and talking to me about the many issues in their lives, the students became more aware of and were able to verbalise more personal reasons for their return. Robson (1993), maintains that listening, hearing and empathy create a situation in which people feel safe and comfortable, and are able to be reflective and talk freely:

> People often derive considerable satisfaction from talking about what they are doing to a disinterested but sympathetic ear. Taking part in a study can often lead to respondents reflecting on their experience in a way they find helpful. (Robson, 1993, p.297)

The students advanced a range of reasons, both practical and personal for their return to education. These reasons are not mutually exclusive and in fact clearly interface with one another in many ways. Whatever the reasons given by the students, it seems to me that a central issue is that the women are using education as a vehicle to change at least some aspects of their identity. It must be pointed out though that few of the students used the actual term 'identity'; this is simply a convenient conceptual basket which I have used to encompass the changes in themselves which the women were describing. The next chapter therefore briefly outlines and examines the concept of identity and the social influences on the identities of both women and men in our society.

3 Identity and education

The role of education in the women's desire to re-shape at least a part of their identity was evident in a number of ways in all their accounts, but was made particularly explicit by Sheila and Jenny, whose stories are told in later chapters. They both emphasised a need to be recognised as individuals in their own right:

> Sheila: I must say that independence is very strong, but also an identity is very very important. The period when I were not working and I were just a wife, I would never say that ... I need that identity and independence.

> Jenny: You lose your identity. You stop being a person when you get married ... I was called Rick's mum, or Trev's wife. And you want to stand on a pedestal and shout, 'look at me - there's me here. I am somebody if you'd take notice'.

Identity could be defined as the characteristics by which individuals and groups recognise themselves and are recognised by others. It is a sense of who we are and where we belong in society, and includes factors such as our sex and gender, race and ethnicity, class, physical, psychological and mental attributes, and where we live, both in a neighbourhood sense and in a broader sense, in terms of our nationality. Clearly, there is no single characteristic which makes up our identity, but a multiplicity of elements which may be divided broadly into biological and social influences.

Both Jenny and Sheila emphasise the social influence on their biological identities as women. This mirrors the debate on the relative influence of biology and society on our identity which has existed for many years and is ongoing. There is now some general acceptance that both 'nature' and 'nurture' are influential in our development, with the relative emphasis moving between the two as the debate develops.

Psychologists such as Eysenck (1967) focus on the biological and genetic aspects of our identity. Eysenck argues that our personality, which is closely aligned with our identity, is biologically rooted and genetically determined. This physiological base will influence the way in which individuals deal with the social situations in which they find themselves. One cannot argue that biological influences are not an intrinsic part of our identity. For example, our hair, eye and skin colour, our height, our age and our reproductive structure are genetically determined and influence the way we see ourselves and others and the way we are seen by others. In terms of our gender identity, we are defined as men and women biologically, and in our society, as in most others, these differences are embedded in the culturally expected behaviour of the two groups.

Sociobiologists maintain that gender divisions arise from the natural (and evolutionary) biological differences between women and men in order to ensure the survival of the species. They have advanced a number of explanations for these differences, such as brain construction, endocrinological make-up and/or genetic programming (see for example, Stevens, 1994; Moir and Jessel, 1989; Goldberg, 1979; Dawkins, 1976). As recently as late last century, biological differences were used to justify keeping women out of higher education on the grounds that overtaxing their lesser (than men's) size brain would impair their childbearing capabilities (Sayers, 1982; Hubbard, 1983)!! Goldberg (1979) maintains that male dominance is universal and biological, though it may take different forms, such as male dominance in the upper hierarchies of all institutions, which he calls patriarchy; male dominance in personal and family relationships, which in his terms are psycho-physiological; and male domination in attainment, whatever form it takes (apart from maternal).

The clear message coming from this perspective is that gender differences are rooted in nature and so are an inevitable and unavoidable feature of our existence, legitimising the superior ordination of men and the subordination of women.

Feminists from a range of perspectives have taken issue with this argument. For example, Oakley (1993), drawing on a broad body of ethnographic evidence, argues that gender divisions are socially rather than biologically created. Charles (1993) examines capitalist, socialist and developing societies and concludes that gender divisions are culturally created. Writing from a materialist feminist perspective, Delphy (1984, 1993) reverses the essentialist argument and maintains that patriarchy is not based upon 'natural' differences between men and women, rather, gender divisions exist because of patriarchal domination. It follows then that in a non-patriarchal society, social divisions between women and men would cease to exist.

The students with whom I talked have been given a biological identity as women, but their roles as daughter, mother and wife are affected by the cultural norms of this society and are thus part of their social identity. Clearly there is a mixture here between the individual and the social and many social constructionist writers such as Mead (1934), Cooley (1964, 1962) and Berger and Luckman (1991) maintain that one cannot easily separate the personal from the social. Whilst we are unique individuals, our sense of self is constructed through socialisation and constantly addressed and adjusted in the ongoing social interaction which takes place throughout our lives.

Connell (1987) maintains that gender is a process, not a 'thing' and Jenkins (1996) argues that this is an interactive process between ourselves and others:

> Social identity is our understanding of who we are and of who other people are, and, reciprocally, other people's understanding of themselves and of others (which includes us) ... Identity is a matter of ascription: by individuals of themselves and of individuals by others.
>
> (Jenkins, 1996: 5; 102)

It is these social influences and their impact on women's identity which are addressed in the remainder of this chapter.

The social influences on gender identity

The social aspects of our identity, and particularly gender differences are reinforced from the day we are born and become so much part and parcel of our existence that we may not even be aware of it (Burr, 1998; Jenkins, 1996; Damon and Hart, 1988).

We are classified as male and female according to biological differences at birth. We are dressed differently - if not in the traditional pink for a girl/blue for a boy, any walk around a shop selling clothes for babies will clearly indicate that a male/female market is aimed at. Modern day colours are bright and jazzy, but in general there is a clear distinction between clothes for boys and clothes for girls. Being dressed differently elicits differences in phrases from adults (despite baby features being asexual) such as 'who's going to be a big strong boy then?' and 'isn't she a pretty little girl?' which undoubtedly helps form the emerging self-identity of the child. This is reinforced with toys, jobs around the house, even patterns of freedom and discipline and very frequently, expectations of academic achievement and career. Many contemporary parents deliberately try to avoid the traditional gender-role socialisation, and although some success can be achieved, few parents want their children to be totally different and in addition of course, children are influenced by other relatives as well as friends, and friends' parents.

This situation is often reinforced when children go to school, as the many texts on gendered education have indicated. Although education is seen as a major vehicle in reducing discrimination, there is ample evidence to suggest that gendered inequalities still persist throughout the system (Skelton, 1997; Thorne, 1993; Delamont, 1990; Burchell and Millman, 1989; Serbin, 1984, Stanworth, 1983). Even where the curriculum is equally available to both males and females, institutional practices and peer group pressure may still emphasise gender differences (Draper, 1993; Delamont, 1990; Lees, 1986; Arnot and Weiner, 1987).

It is not an exaggeration to say that by the time they reach minimum school leaving age, the majority of young men and women have been socialised into and have internalised an ideology of gendered differences. In a society where the gender differences are deeply embedded, our identities are hugely influenced by what is seen as 'normal' behaviour for both men and women. As Simone de Beauvoir argues:

> One is not born a woman, but rather, becomes one.
> (de Beauvoir, 1972: 301)

A large part of what is seen as women's 'natural' role has been focused around caring responsibilities. In societies where the dominant ideology is patriarchal and the argument that gender differences exist 'naturally' are influential, women's happiness and fulfilment is seen, by both men and women, to be located in caring for others (Seidler, 1994; Delphy and Leonard, 1992; Rich, 1977; Delphy, 1984) which then influences their position in both the private world of the home and the public world of work, with women taking the primary responsibility for domestic and caring roles within the home and also being located primarily within the service and caring industries in the world of paid work.

Walby (1986, 1989, 1990) expands the public/private dichotomy and looks at the different levels and the different areas in which patriarchy operates to influence gender identities in western industrialised societies. She defines patriarchy as:

> A system of social structures and practices in which men dominate,
> oppress and exploit women. (Walby, 1990: 20)

and suggests a system of six interlocking and interrelated structures which constitute a system of patriarchy: family, work, the state, male violence, sexuality and culture. Her theory builds on and extends considerable radical feminist theoretical literature (see for example, Millett, 1970; Firestone, 1974; Rich, 1980; Dworkin, 1981; MacKinnon, 1982; Stacey, 1997).

Although there is now acknowledgement that women's and men's positions are changing (Walby 1997; Walter 1999; Franks 1999; Greer 1999) and women are gaining ground in all areas, particularly education, politics and employment, these changes have not affected all women, and older women particularly are still disadvantaged in the job market with fewer qualifications and thus lower paid and often part time jobs. There is considerable evidence from these writers that we still live in a society where women's and men's roles, both formal and informal is influenced by traditional gender approaches.

There is no doubt that the society in which we live, at all levels, has a great deal of bearing on the way we are seen and see ourselves and cultural and social influences were reflected considerably in the stories of the women with whom I spoke. I have used Walby's six interlocking and interrelated structures as a practical framework within which to illustrate these influences on the students' identity, although clearly from their stories, these areas impact on one another. Walby does not order the areas hierarchically, but in my view, culture is pervasive and could be seen as the umbrella under which the other institutions exist.

Culture

The traditional essentialist approach, rooted in biology, that men and women are basically different, in physical, emotional and psychological make-up is still dominant in our society. Despite considerable moves towards gender equality, this approach still influences the socialisation of men and women into different roles from early childhood through the institutions of the family, education, work, leisure and the media, particularly television, films and magazines. These are instrumental in shaping not only individual identities, but also perceptions of the way others should behave (see among many others: Cameron, 1998, 1992; Sharpe, 1994; Thorne, 1993; Spender and Sarah, 1988; Deem, 1980). Marshment (1997, p. 125) argues that 'Representation is a political issue' - women's lack of power in a patriarchal society subjects them to the control of men. Her arguments parallel those of Smith (1987), who points out that our culture is created, and in any society will reflect the wants and needs, thoughts and ideas of the dominant group, which in a patriarchal society, is largely male.

Other work in this area has concentrated on discourse analysis, following Foucault's (1981) idea that control through language is more insidious and powerful than overt power, although Foucault himself had little to say about gender relations. Radical feminists such as Daly (1986), Spender (1980, 1983) and MacKinnon (1982) see the central issue to be how patriarchal discourses are created and maintained rather than how individuals become socialised and have focused on the different representations of gender in the media. Daly (1978) suggests that patriarchal beliefs are at the core of many religious, medical and cultural practices throughout the world and argues that the solution to this control of women is for them to develop a non-patriarchal language and culture.

Spender (1980) and more recently Cameron (1998, 1992), also highlight the importance of language as a controlling factor. They argue that language is patriarchally structured and in many instances, for example the use of the generic 'he' and 'man', renders women invisible. These terms not only reflect the power of men but also contribute to it. Both writers argue that a patriarchal language structure and gendered patterns of language interaction promote a particular view of both men and women and make it more difficult for women to think outside of this patriarchal structure.

The cultural influences on the lives of the women with whom I spoke were pervasive throughout their lives – influencing their early family life, education, and current roles and responsibilities even for younger students. Colette's story, at the end of this chapter, is a powerful example of cultural influences on her identity and her guilt feelings when considering rejecting her traditional female role.

The cultural controls about which Jenny speaks so passionately later in the book operate at both national and local levels, being closely tied to the area in which she lived. She talked of her frustration of the way in which her role was defined and constrained by neighbourhood values:

> It's attitude ... I don't know whether it's just this area. They were always brought up that the males went to work ... the women have always been there for the families, they've always had the home to run. It don't matter whether they've laid on the floor, like I lay on the floor and do homework with my kids, but that doesn't make me a good mother. At the end of the day, if my kids have a hot meal, if they're clean when they go to school, if I'm there to pick them up, that makes you accepted by society otherwise you're not accepted, you're like an outcast. Everybody, I don't care who they are, everybody has to conform to society in some ways.

These broader cultural influences are also reflected in effects on identity within the closer institution of the family and the women talked of both past and present experiences.

Family

The students' stories revealed traditional cultural expectations that a primary part of women's identity is located in domestic and caring responsibilities. This is a major consideration for many if not most mature students (Edwards, 1993; McGivney, 1993; Coats, 1989; Woodley et al, 1987). The majority of women appeared to have been raised in households where conventional male-female roles were prevalent, and as Jenkins (1996: 62) argues, influences on our identities in our early years are generally more deeply embedded and central to our thinking than those experienced later. Here, Gloria emphasises her father's attitude towards her mother and the education of girls:

> He was contemptuous of women and expected women to be barefoot, pregnant and at the kitchen sink most of the time. Any hint of education or intelligence was just squashed. You know, you can't have women with brains, they're not there for that.

The attitude of Gloria's father influenced her brother as well:

> My brother, I remember my Mum said, well we laugh about it now, but I remember my Mum saying to Steve 'Can you, er, you know, it's your turn to do the washing up'. And Steve said 'Why should I do it when I've got two sisters in the house?'.

Though this extent of control was not necessarily evident in all cases, most students' childhood and education had been influenced by attitudes and roles which were clearly gendered, reflecting the norms of a dominant patriarchal culture. In the coming chapters, Alison places emphasis on her father's manipulation; Leila married early to get away from her father's control; Petra talks of domestic responsibilities, influenced by the trauma of her mother's alcoholism; Dilys was kept home from school on many occasions to help with the domestic chores. Sheila talks of the links between domestic expectations because she was a female, and her performance at school:

> Sheila: I were brought up very much within the home to fulfil a woman's role and there were strong socialisation processes ... My eldest sister was suffering from post-natal depression ... I was the youngest female and I had to go and look after the children and put them to bed after school ... I didn't say anything because it were

pointless ... my sister needed help with the children ... but I was always getting into trouble (at school).

These patriarchal influences were also very evident in the students' current situation. The majority of them were partnered and had dependent children living at home. Several women were also responsible for elderly relatives, either living with them or nearby. However, most students did not actually perceive child care and domestic chores as difficulties unless they became a major problem: they are usually seen as 'part of my lot' to organise.

Despite her resentment of neighbourhood pressures and her husband's attempts to restrict her to her domestic role, Jenny sees her home, her husband and her children as entirely her responsibility, even though her husband has not been in paid employment for thirteen years:

Trev's hopeless, absolutely ... I'm on call now for t'phone ... in the last six months I bet I've been called out about twelve times - out of lessons. Littlest had his fingers in the door and Trev couldn't even cope with that. The woman looks after the family...

Sheila's domestic arrangement for the care of her sick son were a constant source of stress for her:

... purely and simply Neil was still my responsibility ... it were my responsibility to find somebody. It was never Joe's responsibility but if he was there he would be quite happy about caring for Neil...

Bryony fits together a tight schedule of work, education, domestic chores and caring responsibilities which include her elderly mother. Her husband could see no reason for her return to education and felt that she should get out and get a job - any job - to contribute to the family income.

He didn't really want me to come to college ... so I go home, cook the meals, doing the ironing at the same time, as you do ... then I do my homework at night ... I get very tired ... he says it's my own fault ... I'm punishing myself ... there's no reason for it ... so I don't say I'm tired, I just get on with it ... he sees it as me being totally selfish...

Heather, who has three children is on a full-time course. Her partner is happy for her to do the course, but does little to help:

He agreed I should do something I enjoyed doing, so yeah, he backed me up ... but doesn't do anything practically to help. He don't do anything in t'house, he wouldn't know where to start, he's terrible, but I suppose I've made him like it, I've carried on where 'is mother left off ...

Me mam used to tell 'im to put t'kettle on if I were busy wi' kids, but he used to say 'That's what I pay 'er for'. 'Bloody pay her?' me mam used to say, 'you don't bloody pay 'er for nothing' but he meant it really - he didn't think that were 'is job ... an' I get so tired an' I get ratty with the kids ...

Generally speaking the women did not question that they have to work round their domestic commitments, whatever they might be, choosing institutions, courses and timetables to fit in, rather than vice versa, although they do talk about the conflicts created by demands on their time at particular times of the year like Christmas and birthdays. Many of them told me too that their employment opportunities were limited because of their caring roles.

Work

In the world of paid work, women on average, earn less than men; are engaged less in paid work than men; have more part-time, temporary and less secure employment than men and do different jobs from men (Social Trends, 1999; Reskin and Padavic, 1994; Lewis, 1992; Pillinger, 1992; Hakim, 1979). There is a clear interface here with the domestic division of labour and evidence of the cultural influence on women's roles. As Jenkins (1996, p.61) argues, our opportunities are frequently influenced by our social identities. Women in the public sphere are primarily located in the caring and service industries, which is not only a reflection of their caring and servicing role in the home but also a reinforcement of it.

Although most of the students were not in employment, there was some evidence from my research data of the links between work, women's perceived gendered roles and their identity. For example, Frances and Jenny did not work outside the home when they left school because they were pregnant, and their current domestic situation also limits their employment opportunities. When Sheila became pregnant before she was married, the firm for whom she worked, which also operated a marriage bar, was not prepared to employ a visibly pregnant woman. When she returned to work two evenings a week with the youth service, her part-time work had to fit around her responsibility for the care of her son.

Ursula told us in the previous chapter that she trained both as a nurse and as a medical secretary and gave up this latter job to return to education. She links her experiences in employment with gender differences:

I think it's because you're a woman and because you're a nurse or a secretary. Definitely. If you had more males in nursing and in secretarial you wouldn't get treated that way. If they were the people that were the breadwinners, they wouldn't treat you that way.

It is also worth noting here that with the exception of Netta and Annabel, all the students who had been in employment, worked in traditionally female occupations in the caring and service industries. All of them finished full-time work when they became pregnant, and where they did return to work, the job was often part-time with no security and of a lower status than before. Nola told me initially that she was aiming for a degree because she did not want to go back into the same clerical work but lower down the scale, which she felt was inevitable, having been out of the job market for a few years. Wanda had considerable difficulty when she wished to return to work:

I did actually try to get back to work full time and this is where I found very surprisingly the prejudice against women with children. I couldn't get a full time job even though I was applying for jobs that were well within my capabilities.

Even though the situation is changing, and women make up nearly half of the workforce in the UK, family responsibilities are regarded by employers as having a different impact on the lives of women and men; disadvantaging women but being seen as stabilizing for male workers. These attitudes are located in the traditional biological approach to identity – that women's 'natural' role is nurturing and caring, and this is linked with the way in which sexuality has been defined for both women and men.

Sexuality

Sexuality is the terrain, the domain in which both men and women come to define themselves in terms of a taken-for-granted gender identity. (Brittan and Maynard, 1984, p.94)

The schools of thought in this area are divided into those who believe that sexuality is an instinct or drive present in all human beings, i.e. an innate part of our identity – an essentialist view, and those who consider it to be socially constructed – that is, a learned part of our identity. The former typically follow a Freudian analysis, others orient towards the second explanation. See for example, Richardson, 1997; Connell, 1995, 1987; Butler, 1990; Walby, 1990; Weeks, 1990; Foucault, 1981; Jackson, 1978; all of whom highlight the cultural focus on essentialism.

The social influence on their sexual identity was reflected in students' stories of early pre-marital pregnancy and sexist experiences in employment, Some of the women who were pregnant before marriage, talked of their feelings of shame and the stigma attached to their condition. Goffman (1968) terms this a 'spoiled' identity whereby some people have power to shape our identity, then treat us according to the label which has been attached. This was particularly highlighted by Bryony:

> I felt so ashamed of myself ... and I'd brought shame on the family ... because to have sex before marriage, I was made to feel absolutely dirty. When I went to the clinic they still called your name as 'Mrs' so again you got the shame thing ...

Alison too talks about the shame, but also about her father's attitude:

> I'd told my mum and she was fine about it, and he (her father) went up the wall. For the whole of the eight months he never spoke to me, not two words ... I was so disappointed with myself becoming an unmarried mother ... you can tell a lie and your lies will not get caught out, but you get pregnant and it grows in front of you for eight, nine months ...

Netta chose to move into a non-traditional area of work, and discovered that the social interpretation of her identity, accepted by both males and females on the course, led to differential treatment on her engineering course:

> There were quite a few girls on the YTS and they all tended to get grouped together and I didn't like that very much I didn't want to get stuck with them because they were just there for laugh. They didn't take it as seriously as I did and they weren't as good at it as I was and I would rather have been with the boys or teenagers doing the proper engineering stuff instead of pratting about ...

> The students with special needs and the females were all put to one side and that really irritated me, they stopped it after a bit but it really irritated me that ...

This type of sexism was also experienced by Annabel. She is the only remaining student on the second year of the Women's Motor Vehicle course, and because of this, she is with second year males. Her experiences may go some way to explaining why the numbers have shrunk so drastically:

> Annabel: They just treat me like I'm so stupid and it's very difficult to fight that all the time ... I just feel all my confidence going ...

Nobody comes near you. All day they ignore you and nobody says anything all day to you, then they don't sign your job sheets because they say they haven't seen what you're doing. This guy stood over me and made me tighten the wheel nuts with a torque wrench. I thought he was having me on but it was obvious he was going to force me to do it. I thought later I should have said 'OK, now I've done this will you teach me something proper?' but I thought he'd just go in the locker room or whatever and have a good laugh about how he got the woman to do the wheel nuts to-day ...

Annabel also experienced considerable sexual harassment from both students and male staff members:

They won't sign the register unless you're in a classroom at a particular time. You have to stand around in a really crowded room with about forty blokes, you're the only woman, for ages 'til they call out your name. So I usually like to go late on when nobody else is there and I just say, look I'm here. And he'd say, 'I'm not going to sign you in unless you're there at this time'. So I was not noted down for the one morning - or they'd refuse to sign out worksheets on the same day or make a real problem out of it.

One time I was in the workshop and somebody, some bloke, bumped into me and the other said how he wanted to screw me and then they started talking about whether he would like screwing ... here and in the car, and all this kind of thing. The tutor was right there and he didn't stop it. So I left the workshop ... The tutor was standing next to them and I said to him, 'You heard that didn't you?' He said, 'I swear to you I didn't hear anything'.

Annabel was stepping outside of the cultural expectations of a woman's role and the treatment she experienced reflects both the powerful patriarchal control and the power of the essentialist influence on our identity whether we choose to conform to the label or not. The abuse which she experienced links sexuality and male violence.

Male violence

Generally speaking, discussion of male violence against women has focused on physical violence associated with a few psychologically disturbed men, perceived as abnormal. This view is not borne out by evidence of rape and domestic violence which according to the statistics, is far more prevalent than could be accounted for by being simply the acts of a few disturbed men (CSO, Social Trends, 1999; Nussbaum, 1996; Lees, 1994; Mooney, 1993;

Kelly, 1988; Hanmer and Saunders, 1984; London Rape Crisis Centre, 1984; Russell, 1984).

A number of students talked of physical and/or psychological violence and its effects on their identity. Some of them are mentioned here briefly, but the links between violence, education and identity are discussed in greater detail in later chapters. Claire, for example, told me that she had had a nervous breakdown after experiencing marital violence. Gerry's sexual identity was violently defined, through sexual abuse by her brother when she was a child. Her story tells of a major impact on her identity:

> I ran away from home while I was at school a couple of times ... I tried to commit suicide twice ... I didn't know where I was as a person or what I wanted to do with life. I was just aimlessly going along from one thing to another ... messed me up completely – totally affected my attitude and the way I looked at things. I still do to a certain extent walk around with this huge chip on my shoulder...

Jenny told me of her husband's change from physical to psychological violence, and the effect it has had on her. She is awaiting counselling because of her husband's attempts to control all aspects of her life:

> My husband's getting really nasty just now. I was actually a battered wife at one time ... I'm four foot ten and Trev's six foot four, so there's a big difference in size ... I'm good at putting a front on. Luckily I've never broken down here, but I've got to see the CPN (Community Psychiatric Nurse) 'cos I collapsed in the doctor's. I was actually a battered wife at one time, now he's gone from physical to mental. He doesn't realise he's doing it, but it's the same type of thing ... I'm getting to nearly screaming stage at times ...

Deidre talked about the effect of being told for many years by her (ex) husband that she was the stupid one of the family:

> Well, sometimes in married life you'll get your partner that he's always telling you that you're the idiot of the family and you can't do this and you can't do that - and after about nineteen years you eventually believe it - you know?

The physical violence which Della experienced also affected her psychologically:

> When Jon was born the physical violence started ... I've had my legs broken, I've had black eyes, I've had my teeth knocked out, my lips split ... I was trying to question – 'what have I done?' I'd find

something I'd done to justify what he done to me - I didn't do this
right or I said that wrong or his tea wasn't ready, silly stupid things ...

The police attitude towards her when she called them in reflects the
state's view of a woman's identity when she is married:

He went into t'kitchen, he got a hammer, he smashed every stick of
furniture in the house, every single bit. That's the time I ended up
with broken fingers and a split lip ... I threw him out. I locked the
doors, called the police. They came and it was, well it's done with,
it's a domestic and, you know, a typical male attitude. They couldn't
see what we had been through and they were going to let him get
away with it again.

The State

Over the years, much government legislation and many legal decisions have
both reflected and reinforced women's identities in all areas of their lives
and its influence can be seen within the areas of work, family, sexuality and
violence. The above quote from Della illustrates this and the police
treatment of Vida's sexuality, which is discussed later in the book reflects
the state's reinforcement of gender identities.

When women are not present in any large numbers in the decision-
making process, despite the recent increase in women MPs, and they cannot
therefore bring the same power to bear as men on the outcome of decisions,
the resolution of which tend to be patriarchal in nature. An example of this
is the denial of custody to lesbian mothers simply because they are lesbian
which can be seen as a reflection of patriarchal, heterosexual ideology,
though this is now changing. Secondly, the laws on rape and domestic
violence have been slow to change and are still largely discriminatory
against women. It is only as recently as 1990 that the law on marital rape
was changed, and even now in rape cases, the law allows for the differential
examination of past sexual histories, with the sexual history of the victim
being examined as part of the defence whereas an examination of the sexual
history of the defendant is not allowed (Lees, 1994, 1997). A clear link here
between sexuality, violence and the role of the state.

A point which I feel is crucial to the position of women is the
patriarchal nature of the welfare state, established in the 1940s. The welfare
benefits structure particularly was based on the ideology of a 'middle-class
ideal family type' which predominated in our society from the end of last
century (Poster, 1978; Barrett, 1980), with a male breadwinner and
dependant wife and children, despite the fact that there is a disjuncture
between this ideal and the actual household structure of many families.

Many trades unions though, in the first half of this century, based their claim for higher wages on the principle of a 'family wage' for men (Wilson, 1977, 1983; Land, 1985) and even women's trade unions went along with this (Boston, 1980). Given the dominance of this ideology therefore, it is not surprising that welfare benefit legislation should be based on the same principles.

In a later chapter, Jenny talks about the limitations which the benefit structure imposed on her education:

> I'm a non-person, I've no money of my own, I'm not on any computer for any benefit 'cos it goes in my husband's name ... I don't exist ... he gets £20 a week for having me ... I come here (to the neighbourhood centre) 'cos it's just down the road and everything's free ... but if I want anything, I have to ask 'im for it ... I can't go to (college) 'cos of the fares ... there's all sorts I'd love to do but can't afford to do ... because of t'benefit trap ...

Although the grant structure for higher education is now changing, the basic premise remains the same: the grant is determined by personal circumstances, which includes a woman's marital status. If she is married, and has not earned sufficient money outside the home in the last three years to meet independent status, her grant is assessed on the basis of her husband's income.

When Sheila entered higher education, she discovered that her grant was based on her husband's income. She expressed a great deal of resentment, especially since Joe did not make up the difference between the state's estimate of her needs as a student and what she was actually getting. This of course undermines the state's assumption of a male provider who will share his income or provide fully for his partner and reinforces women's primary role in the home.

> I don't get a full grant, Joe pays for my petrol and books, but I don't get what he should pay. I find it frustrating that, I don't think that it's fair that I'm not eligible for a full grant. I think what is really frustrating for me is being discriminated against because we actually have a marriage licence. There's those with long term partners, but they haven't got a marriage licence, and they get a full grant.

Whether a woman is even considered for a grant is dependent upon her husband filling in the earnings declaration. Rhona's husband refused to complete the grant form when she was offered a place at university, so she will get no maintenance grant at all. If her husband chose not to support her, she would not be able to go - as she says:

My fees are paid but I won't get a grant ... because first of all John doesn't want to fill in all the forms, right, he said 'It's you who's going to University not me ...

For the women at Further Education level, the grant is discretionary, and therefore in the current economic climate, non-existent, unless the course is sponsored - for example, by the European Social Fund. Free tuition is mostly only associated with full-time courses, unless students are in receipt of certain state benefits, which most married women are not, and care for children or elderly dependents must generally be paid for.

The implication from the state's treatment of these women is that they do not have identities as individuals because they are married. There also seems to be some contradiction here between the state's avowed commitment to encouraging mature students back into education, and the practical underpinning of that commitment. Nevertheless many women do return to education and succeed at a range of levels which can be seen as a clear attempt by them to change some aspect of their lives and to take control over at least a part of the way in which their identity has been defined.

Agency

This chapter has discussed primarily the social influences on our identity, using Walby's (1990) concept of six interlocking and overlapping structures as an organisational framework. The discussion has been illustrated by verbatim extracts from the students' stories which have provided evidence that the women returners with whom I talked have been controlled and constrained to various degrees by the patriarchal nature of society. However, this does not mean that they have no agency - no control over the way in which their identities have been and continue to be defined. Their return to education has, in part, been about changing at least a part of their identity. Returning to learning is of course in itself an example of the women acting in their own interests, sometimes in spite of a great deal of opposition and some difficulty, as the stories in the coming chapters will illustrate.

The gains which the students were talking about in the previous chapter, apart from the obvious paper qualifications, were fulfilment, an increasing confidence, a positive self-image and independence, all of which can be put under the umbrella term of identity. One or two students in fact did mention a 'different' identity. If we look at the converse of these gains - low confidence, lack of fulfilment, dependence and poor self-image and link them back into the women's stories, it can be argued that the patriarchal structure of society was instrumental either directly, or indirectly, in influencing these negative aspects of the students' identity.

Our agency though is constrained by the society in which we live, and this chapter ends with the story of one student, Colette, which illustrates beautifully the conflict between the structural constraints on her identity, her resistance to this and the tension between the two.

A case study - Colette

Colette is 31, married with two children aged four and six. She is enrolled on an EU funded course at a local college. Her traumatic experiences started with the birth of her first child, a son. It was a difficult pregnancy and a painful birth, culminating in a caesarean section. The child was a difficult and fretful baby who did not sleep and she became exhausted. She blamed her husband for 'giving me this problem' and her relationship with him deteriorated despite the fact that she acknowledges that he tried to be supportive. This he did in practical terms, but saw the problem as lying with her rather than the baby and did not recognise her need for emotional support:

> My son was awful, still is, but that's me, he was awful as a baby - never slept, cried constantly. I felt like throwing him on t'bed a few times. I had a problem with the birth and everything. He was breach and I had to have a caesarean and it was quite a lot to add to but my husband said it was me and that's like a red rag to a bull. It just got worse and worse and I still don't get on with my son, even though, how can I say, he's not a horrible child he's good and everybody likes him at school ... I wouldn't say I blamed him for what he did to me but it was a bad time and me and my husband didn't get on at all.

> I was awful and in the end Paul had a word with his mum and said 'Look you'll have to talk to her', because he was at the end of his tether and he said he used to drive round and think 'I daresn't go home, what's she going to be like?', which I can see. At that time, it was 'you give me this baby'. It's just like your husband that gets it and I let it all out and she (her mother-in-law) didn't understand because she'd had three wonderful children - like they do.

> I've had another, because I didn't want just one. We had a girl and she was completely different ... she's my favourite and he isn't. I've told Paul that but he just says 'You can't feel like that', but you do, you can't help how you feel can you?

I asked Colette why she had chosen to return to education when she did:

> Well, he'd started nursery. If it'd been her, I think I wouldn't have come. It was like 'he's going to nursery, there's somebody who can have him', because I don't really want him. I know I shouldn't say that, but perhaps that's the feeling. I mean, I don't want him, I mean all the time ... Paul wanted me to do it ... because he knew how fed up and bored I was at home and I suppose how nasty I was ... I get on better with the kids and I get on better with my husband as well because you tend to take it out on them don't you?

I think an interesting issue is raised here – Colette's relationship with her husband appeared to be fine until the birth of her first child which seems to have had a major detrimental effect on it. However, he did try to be supportive and encouraged her to return to education as a possible way of easing her problems at home. When Colette went to college the situation with her husband appeared to improve, but then seem to be deteriorating for a different reason:

> ... sometimes I could just be on my own ... at the moment we are going through a bad patch, we just don't seem to see each other because I'm busy and he's working late ... We are drifting apart and I don't know whether to blame me changing or what, but it's not good at the moment. I met up with some old colleagues where I used to work last week and everybody noticed that I was more confident basically, so is it for the good or not? Am I getting over the being married, having kids stage? Is the next step, like these you read in the paper, mum leaves home and disappears forever? I know this is awful, but I see myself on my own and that's really bad because of the kids ... 'cos the kids should stay with mum ... but if I'm honest, I would say that I see myself on my own ...

Although the relationship does seem to be deteriorating, it seems she is better able to cope with it. Colette was almost thinking aloud at this point:

> I don't think I'd ever get married again ... I don't know what it is, I just know it's a big turning point for me at the moment, which way to go and what to do. But I think Paul feels the same, I don't think it's just me, there's a big gap between us and it's not just from me it's from him as well. So what's going to happen in t'future I don't know. I don't how to bridge that gap, it seems to be getting wider ... I think I don't want to, but then I do, I don't want to and then I think I

should. I should rather than I do, because there's the kids involved. I don't blame college but it has changed my life so really if it come to a divorce or something I would have to say that's what really happened ... we've just drifted apart ...

It seems there are many issues with which Colette is wrestling at the moment. She is recognising that she is changing and developing as a person and this change is causing some inner conflict. There are a number of ways in which education plays a part in her story: as with many other students, her course is therapeutic:

I was fed up at home ... I got where I was a bit miserable and not wanting to do anything or go anywhere. Now, I'm just a different person, ask anyone, they can see the change in me. I don't think I'm perhaps the old Colette that I was before the kids came along, because they change your life, but I really feel like I'm 21 again.

She is also desperately trying to find an identity outside of her domestic and caring role:

I wanted to do something for myself, yes for myself. I didn't want to be a mum with two kids. I wanted to do something for myself and not she's somebody's mum and that's Paul's wife type of thing and I must admit I've become Colette Smith again which was my maiden name and not Mrs Brown, who is just a mum and Paul's wife. Does that make sense? I do love my kids but I don't think I want to be a mum any more, are you with me?

I must admit I've got where I'm not bothered any more about housework, whereas I was one to. If there was a bit of fluff there I'd get t'hoover out, I did take a lot of pride in the home. I think I'm just not bothered any more. Like yesterday, he said 'It could do with hoovering up in here' and I said 'Yes, it could' and looked at him as if to say 'get t'hoover out then' ... He didn't, but that doesn't bother me, whereas at one point we used to be bickering about that as well. But it's true, things like that do get left ... other things are more important aren't they now? I mean I sat there and did some homework instead of hoovering up.

Colette appears to be wrestling with what she wants and what she feels society expects of her. I felt that for a large part of the interview she was thinking aloud and attempting to remedy a negative self-image she had of herself because of the way she felt. She has conflicting views of herself as a career woman, as a wife and as a mother:

I do think I've changed ... I haven't really been a career woman have I, but I think I'm going that way. At the end of it I do want a good job I don't really want the university education that this course leads to. I mean I say that now, but perhaps in another six months, I might change my mind and decide to go because I'm surprising myself with the results that I'm getting - 70 and 80 percent. I always thought that I was thick, well you do don't you, I always did at school...

She raised the question 'Is it college that's done that to me or is it me?' but does recognise that there was a desire in her to do something outside of the home:

I didn't sort of think 'Is it too much hassle to do it?' There was something saying 'You are going to do it for yourself, for you, you're going to do it', and I think that's what started it off really. I would never give it up even if I failed things. I just want it.

Her conflict over the children was clear. She recognised that whilst it may be socially acceptable for her to leave her husband, it was not so for her to dislike and maybe leave the children:

It's hard telling people you don't get on with your son especially when he's only little. It's not acceptable. If I don't get on with my husband I should leave him and take the kids with me, because that's what happens - the kids stay with mum. What frightens me I think, after a couple of months, would I change? You don't know till you do it. If I could like be away from them for like a few months I might think 'I do want my kids, I'm not bothered about my husband', you know what I mean? But you can't do that can you, you can't do that to the kids? Really. It's tough isn't it, especially when their only so young ...

Everything that Colette told me was linked in with a strong desire for both social and economic independence:

You do struggle on one wage with two small children, you want to do things you can't. But also it is the independence part of it as well, you don't want to be the little wife at home any more. I don't think most women do now. I think my age group is having four or five years at home and they've had enough. A lot of people I worked with went back to work straight away. Sometimes I regret that, I wish that I'd done that ... and also I want a social life as well. I don't know whether that comes along with the college bit, but I'm wanting to have the relaxation part of it on my own really, going out with my friends instead of my husband and sometimes I think 'Is that wrong?'

But then I think, 'No, he goes out, he goes out with football, why shouldn't I?' He doesn't say no you can't go but if there's not much money in the kitty, obviously we have words about it, which is right, but I find that we are drifting apart and I don't know whether to blame me changing or what.

There are many aspects to Colette's story. Since being in education, she has gained in confidence and self-awareness and appears to be fighting conflicting emotions, many of them influenced by social pressure, to create a new identity for herself. The guilt feelings she verbalises are again influenced by the social norms she feels she is contravening. She sees herself as deviant, almost morally evil in that she is contemplating leaving her children, but at the same time she is fighting the constraints and the identity which she sees as being imposed by her marriage and family.

The influence of patriarchy on Colette's life and feelings is clear, but it is not a total influence and there is unmistakable evidence of agency. She is aware that what she is planning to do is not what women are normally expected to do in this society. Whilst this is a reflection of the power of patriarchal influence, Colette seems to be determined to carve out a new identity for herself and education appears to be a vehicle she is using.

Summary

Identity then develops through a mixture of biology, socialisation and agency. We are all influenced by the patriarchal nature of the society in which we live, and Walby's six structures have been a useful framework within which to examine the effects on our identity, highlighting the overlapping and interlocking nature of the way in which those structures work to reinforce gender divisions and influence our self perceptions.

However, the research data indicates that although patriarchy may well provide the backcloth against which our identities are shaped, agency, at least on a micro level, is very evident in the everyday lives of mature women returners to education. Within that overall framework they are working, albeit within constraints, to influence the way their identities may have been defined and are seen by others and the way in which they see themselves.

The need to change at least part of their identity is reflected in the stories of the majority of the women I spoke with, but was particularly so for those who told me of traumatic experiences, either current or past. The coming chapters examine the links which the students make both directly and indirectly between these experiences, identity and education.

4 The impact of major life events or changes

A number of students told me of events which had been unexpected and/or had created a major change in their lives, which had made each of them re-assess her life and needs and what she wanted to do. For example, Deidre talked of divorce and a major operation and Liz told me of serious injury. Joy, Olga and Leila talked about their redundancy from jobs which they found less than fulfilling, which gave them the opportunity to fulfil a long-held, if not always verbalised desire to return to learning and change at least a part of their identity. For Leila, redundancy was one of a number of problems she faced, and her story, which she tells last in this chapter, introduces some of the topics which are included in the next. For Heather it was the death of both her parents within a year which made her consider her position and return to education.

Heather

Heather is 39, married with three young children. She had a basic gendered education, leaving school at 15 with no official qualifications to work initially in routine office work, then in retailing. She is enrolled on a full-time EEC funded women's technology course.

Heather's parents were both retired from full-time work when her children were born, and took a regular and active interest in their upbringing, with her father visiting every day to help with the children whilst Heather worked part-time in a local factory. Her father became ill with a brain tumour in September 1991 and died late on Christmas Eve the same year. She talked of the dilemma of having to choose between staying with her father at the hospital, knowing that his death was imminent, and going home to be with her children at Christmas. She told me that her mother persuaded her to return home and she still carries guilt feelings about not being with her father when he died:

Heather: he died in St. Lukes, and we were all up there from dinner

47

time. And my mum sent me home, 'cos she said, 'You know your dad, he'd want you to be wi' kids, and there's nowt you can do anyway. You can come again tomorrow'. And I think deep down I knew that I weren't going to see him again, but I were torn. Because I know my dad would have wanted me to be at home with t' kids because my kids were like a big part of my dad's life. I mean, he used to idolise them, particularly t' big one, and so I were torn. But I went home, I went home. I've got a lot of regrets about that because I weren't with him when he died.

And I were really horrible to my mum, because I blamed her. Now two years on I know it weren't her fault, it were nobody's fault what were the matter with him, but you just lash out ...

Heather's guilt feeling were compounded when her mother became ill with a brain tumour three weeks after the death of her father and was hospitalised, dying in the following December. She felt much responsibility for her mother's condition since she agreed to the unsuccessful operation:

... then three weeks after, my mum collapsed with the same thing and we had to decide whether my mum had t' operation or not ... she ended up a cabbage and she was in hospital for ten months. Although you do what you think's right at the time ... you can't help thinking 'I've done this to her. She's like this because I've said yes for her to have t' operation'. She just, she didn't know anybody, she didn't speak, she couldn't, she couldn't swallow, she were on a ventilator, she ... it were just awful, her being like that.

It is not only the loss of both parents, but also the circumstances in which they died, which was difficult for Heather:

So really, for fifteen months, from September 1991 through to December 1992, we visited t' hospital every day - with the exception of about three weeks between my dad dying and my mum collapsing. It's been hard, and particularly for me ... by the time I had my kids my parents had retired, so my life and my kids lives sort of revolved round my parents. They were always there for me you know? If ever I needed them for anything. So it's been hard, it's been terrible in fact, bearing in mind we'd only lost my dad three weeks before - and we'd nursed my dad through dying ... he were just dying slowly, and when you've got to sit back and there's nothing you can do, it's hard.

Heather's painful experiences made her take stock of her life.

I just couldn't cope with what was happening to my dad and I was taken ill myself. And I think I just sort of sat back and took a good look at myself and I thought, 'Well there's got to be more for me than this, this job'.

She makes two clear links between her story and education. One is the long-term goal of self-fulfilment through a more satisfying job:

At that time I were thirty seven, and I thought, 'well, my kids are at school, and I've got, like, five days a week - from nine o'clock while three o'clock - to do something for myself'. So I thought 'well, I've got another twenty odd years really, that I can work, and why not try and do something that I enjoy doing?' If I've got a chance of getting a better job, and doing something that I enjoy doing, then it's got to be a lot better for me, and for the rest of them in long run. I started January 1993, so me mum had just died, just before I started ...

Heather's other link with education is therapeutic:

I really don't know what I'd have done if I hadn't got this to look forward to and to occupy me. I just sort of sunk myself into it. I've got this big hole in my life and I'm also trying to protect ' kids 'cos I know they're hurting and when your kids are hurting you hurt, and its even worse because you can't do owt about it ... maybe I didn't grieve enough ... Sometimes I feel I'm going crackers - in my head'.

Her recent trauma tended to colour Heather's interpretation of most of what we discussed and I could not seem to find a way round this, which is not surprising really since her parents appear to have been a major supporting element in her life. Her painful experiences have clearly been influential in her assessment of the way she sees herself and what she wants from her life. A brain tumour had a similar influence on the next student, but for Deidre, it was her own operation.

Deidre

Deidre is 48, divorced with one son who lives at home periodically, and is enrolled on the same course as Heather. She had an elementary, gendered, gender-segregated education and left school at 15 to work in retailing. She has not worked since her marriage at 21. Significant factors in Deidre's decision to return to education appear to be her divorce in 1986 and an operation for a brain tumour in 1988:

I'm divorced and consequently I was unemployed and there was no money coming in. When I left school I had no qualifications whatsoever. I haven't got any skills for anything and jobwise I can't do much anyway, you know? I get maintenance from my ex-husband, if you can call it that, 10p a year. I'm afraid I told him where to put it.

Also in 1988 I had an operation for a brain tumour - and people tend to treat me with kid gloves. You know? 'Since she's had this operation there must be something wrong with her, you know, it's affected her brain and she can't learn properly'. So I'm really doing it for myself.

Deidre makes three links with education. The one she emphasises is the testing of her ability:

Deidre: Well, for long enough now I've wanted to come back into education. I've been unemployed for quite a long time now and I wanted to really know if I could actually do anything academic-wise. That was my main one ... I wanted to know how well I'd done up to Christmas before I applied. From what I can gather, I'm not doing too bad really. You see, all the subjects that I'm taking, I've never done before, so it's a bit of a problem that way for me, you know? ... With not knowing anything, it makes it doubly difficult for me to get my credits.

As Deidre said in chapter two, her return to learning is very tentative, not wanting to take the next step before she is sure that she can do it. Testing her ability is also tied up with confidence, and although Deidre's confidence is growing, her hold on it is somewhat tenuous:

The confidence is my problem, the lack of it.

There's lots of areas I could improve on, but I'm a bit more confident than when I first started on this course. I mean, if I'd wanted to ask somebody anything in a shop or anywhere I used to creep in and this little voice used to come out - now I'll just walk in and ask. You know, if we get set an assignment and we've got to collect things I will go in and it doesn't bother me as much now.

Finally, the way Deidre sees herself is also changing. Both her confidence and her self image appear to have been negatively affected by her marriage:

Well, sometimes in married life you'll get your partner that he's always telling you that you're the idiot of the family and you can't do this and you can't do that - and after about nineteen years you eventually believe it - you know? And you think, 'Well happen I can't do this and I can't do that', you know?

So it's only really since I've separated from him and also I've had the operation that I've thought, 'Well why can't I do this and why can't I do that?' and I'm beginning to see myself differently.

This student was very quiet and I found it very difficult to get her to talk in a relaxed way. After the tape was switched off, she said that I'd probably got much more interesting things from some of the other women who had husbands and small children to care for and homes to run. Her reticence was not, I felt, due to unwillingness, rather a lack of confidence which led her to assume that she didn't really have anything important to say. However, there are clear indications from what Deidre says about her confidence and a more positive self-image, that she is getting much more from her course than just a paper qualification.

Unlike Deidre, the next student has only recently left the job market, but the two students are similar in that Liz is also beginning to see herself differently.

Liz

Liz is aged 35, married with a young daughter. She had a basic education and left with few qualifications. She took a secretarial course and worked as a secretary for three years before becoming a nurse. She is enrolled on the second year of a full-time social science access course at a local college and has a conditional offer at one of the universities in the area to study history. She qualified as a nurse in 1981 but had a serious spinal operation in 1986 and had to give up nursing, much against her desire, last year. She told me that it was very likely that she would be wheelchair bound in a few years' time. I asked her why she had chosen to come back into education:

... forced upon me in a way. I qualified as a nurse in 1981, and then in 1986 I had an operation to remove one of my lumbar discs - and at that time I chose to go back to nursing - which really wasn't the cleverest thing to do. Then, at the beginning of last year I started to have trouble again with my back and I had to go to bed for a week, and it frightened me, I think. I knew I'd got to come out of nursing eventually, so I thought about coming back to school but I think it isn't until something like becoming ill and having to go to bed, and realising that this is the time that it's got to stop. And plus my GP said 'you know, you're not doing yourself any favours, eventually you'll get worse if you don't stop now'. That's what really made me think it was time to come back to school.

I asked Liz why she had chosen education:

Liz: For a long while I was thinking what I was going to do. If this hadn't happened with my back I would have stayed in nursing because it's what I really wanted to do from leaving school. I felt like I'd been retired too soon ... I thought I'd got to use this nursing knowledge for something ... but I came on this course, I thought I might find something else (and) it develops your personal life as well.

When I asked Liz what she meant by this last remark, she told me that she felt she had changed considerably whilst she had been on the course. She makes three key links with education: independence, confidence and identity.

Her independence is not of the economic variety, since she told me that if her husband wasn't supportive, she would not be able to do the course. She is now financially dependent upon him, for the first time since their marriage and she will not get a grant at university because of the level of his income. She told me that this was not a problem but she doesn't like it, although at this stage she doesn't see how she can do anything about it. She has however become independent in other ways:

I've met an awful lot more friends here that I'm far more friendly with. Before, his friends were my friends and the parties and the things, it was all based around his work. So coming here, breaking away, I've made an awful lot more friends of my own and got a bit of a social life going I think.

Her confidence has also grown:

I don't put up with things like I used to. I think I probably stand up for myself a bit better now than I ever did before ... and, it's like having the confidence to stand up and talk ... at the beginning I would have said no because I'm just not that sort of person, but it doesn't worry me now.

Liz's identity was clearly tied up with being a nurse - a job which she obviously enjoyed and reluctantly gave up. The possibility of being a wheelchair user seemed to play a large part in her thinking, but since she has started the access course, she is able to see beyond this:

I used to worry an awful lot, especially about my back problem, it used to worry me a great deal, looking on the black side I suppose ... You get to this stage and you think well there is something else I can do, and it doesn't end there. I've just been probably looking on the black side.

I asked her why she has chosen the course she planned to take at a local university. Her response links identity and self-fulfilment:

I want to do it because I want to do it. Because it's for me really. I'll worry about what I'm going to do with it when I've got it. If that makes sense?

Liz's major concern seems to have been the loss of her identity as a nurse and potentially as an able-bodied person. She is addressing both these issues through her return to education, but she also talks of benefit through some social independence and an increased confidence. Though Liz gave up her job voluntarily, it seems apparent that she would not have done but for her spinal problem, whereas Joy, Olga and Leila's job losses were involuntary, through redundancy. For all three of them though, a return to education had been something 'at the back of my mind' for some considerable time.

Joy

Joy is studying on the foundation year of a four-year combined studies course which has been franchised out to a local college from one of the nearby universities. She has held a variety of secretarial/ administrative posts all her working life, moving to this area from the south for her partner's education. She supported him financially through his three-year university course and he is now very supportive of her decision to take the opportunity to do a degree course:

I was made redundant at the end of May ... I think if I'd not been made redundant it would still be something that I would do later, something to be forced into really.

Janet: Did you have to be forced into it?

Oh no, I wanted the interest, I could see that it was rewarding and enriches your life in all sorts of ways ... (but) if I hadn't been able to get a grant for this year, I don't know how I would have been able to do it because my partner has a job but we've never earned that much and we've never lived on what he just earned.

Joy went on to tell me that she had been a 'bit of a rebel' at school, and that the mainstream system 'failed in offering the opportunities'. She has taken the opportunity of her redundancy to return to education and gain the qualifications she feels she could have got when she was younger, given the right guidance from her parents and the school. She also told me of her increasing confidence in her academic ability, as did Olga, who was also 'a bit of a rebel' at school:

Olga

This student is 40 and married with three children, all of whom are financially independent. She is doing a full-time science access course at one of the local colleges and has been offered a place on a nursing degree at one of the local universities. She went to grammar school but left at the minimum leaving age with 2 O-levels to work in retailing before becoming pregnant the following year at 16.

> I had a great time in school, but not working! I was told not to even consider coming back in the sixth form. I had a sort of love-hate relationship with the teachers and the head teacher. I think relationshipwise, we got on great as long as they didn't have to teach me! I was a bit lively ...

She has had a chequered work career, though latterly in management posts, and after being made redundant chose this particular course to fulfil a long-held desire to do nursing:

> I was made redundant ... I'd always wanted to go into nursing and it's never, ever been feasible before because I've always needed to be out earning. And suddenly it was possible when the boys were grown up and we can just about manage on one income.

For both Joy and Olga, redundancy was used as the opportunity to change their lives and fulfil long-held ambitions, despite having held quite responsible jobs. Education was seen as the vehicle to do this through gaining better qualifications. Olga emphasised the positive aspects of college life outside the course, and her growing confidence:

> ... the induction was a nightmare ... it was nerves about meeting a lot of people and 'am I capable of doing it'. But after the first week, the feelings Sunday night – being really excited because the following morning was the Monday morning and I couldn't wait to get to college.

Olga and her peers are very supportive of one another and recognised the importance of this:

Well, everybody was in the same boat wasn't they? We've all blown it once in some way and decided to take a totally new start ... it's been brilliant really.

Leila saw her loss of employment as an opportunity to return to education, though she describes her redundancy as a much more painful experience than did either Joy or Olga.

Leila

Leila is 40 years old, partnered and is a full-time student on the foundation year of a four-year science course at a local college, franchised out from one of the universities in the area. She had been working as a computer programmer, but was made redundant the year before she started her course. However, she was very bored with the job and it was a combination of this boredom, her redundancy, the depression which she was experiencing and her age, which made her question what she was doing and the direction she wanted her life to take:

> I've been working for the last twelve years, as a computer programmer, and it was a combination of circumstances, I was made redundant twice within two years, I was finding it extremely difficult to get another job after I was made redundant the first time. A lot of the jobs that I was qualified for, I wasn't even being offered an interview, because the people doing the interviewing were young men - it's a very unfair situation, but rather than try and battle, I thought, 'I'm better off out of it', because to be honest, after ten years of programming, I'd had enough, I was bored with it, 'cause I'd done it. You know, you've written one sales ledger, you've written hundreds of them, they're all the same. There's no challenge left any more when you've done one of everything ...

> ... and because of my age as well, I was having a bit of a mid-life crisis and started thinking, 'What am I doing with my life? There must be some purpose to it. I've got this brain, why don't I start using it? Why don't I prove to myself that I'm capable of doing it?' So there was that at the back of my mind, I was having a couple of spells of depression as well, which I think was to do with the work situation.

Leila addressed this identity crisis by taking an aptitude test at the local careers advisory service and enrolling on her current course, although she does not have a clear career pattern in mind. I asked her why she chose that particular course:

Because I loved chemistry at school, and obviously you do get to know yourself a little bit in 40 years. That's the way my mind works, I've got a logical mind, and it's got to be science subjects rather than non-science, definitely ... In a way, it's an indulgence to do the course, because it's something that I'm interested in. Even if I don't end up getting the right career at the end of it, the course itself is interesting and it's showing me that I am capable of doing it, because I've done quite well so far. No, I haven't got a definite career in mind, so in a way, it's a bit of self-indulgence isn't it?

I asked Leila about her early education and she mentioned her father's attitude as having a major negative influence on her life:

I went to a mixed sex grammar school and I left with seven O-levels when I was sixteen. I thought about the reasons why I left a lot, in the last few years. I actually left to get married. My father told me he didn't think it was a good idea but it didn't stop me. I think the real reason I wanted to get married was because I didn't have a very happy home life, and I was trying to get away from him. We get on alright now, but at the time, I think it was probably the easiest thing for both of us and it was the best excuse possible for leaving home.

I think his plans for me were that I should have stayed on, got my A-levels and gone to university. But knowing what I was like at the time, I probably would have flunked university, I don't think I would have got through it. Very quiet and very shy and I don't think I would have survived being away from home on my own.

Leila told me that her father was very much the controlling force within the family:

Mum didn't have any say in it. Whatever he wanted, she did, she was at home looking after us, that was her place. In some respects, he had a very Victorian attitude towards his marriage, but not towards his children. Well, we were very, very strict. He had some very Victorian attitudes about how to bring up kids, no freedom whatsoever, but as far as education and the prospects were concerned, I could have been a lad. He was a lot less strict with the other two. I think he probably realised he'd gone a bit too far with me, he'd been too strict.

However, Leila's move away from home was not the escape that she had thought it would be - she entered a stultifying marital relationship. Her role was clearly located in the home and she felt isolated, lonely, and frustrated, with most of her friends still in education and no support from her extended family:

> I worked for about six months just after I got married, and then had a baby and that was that! It was a very difficult time really because the feller that I married was probably in the same sort of mode as my father. He wanted somebody to have his meals ready, do all the washing, look after his kids, look after the house, and after twelve months I was bored silly.

> When I went into it, I thought I loved him. You think when you're young and idealist that love conquers everything. Then when you're left there with a toddler and you can't go anywhere, 'cos you're so tied, nobody'll come and baby-sit, I was just so bored, I was taking it out on the kid, I was losing my temper with him. I thought the answer was having another baby, and obviously it just makes things worse. I kept saying to him, 'I'm stagnating, I feel as though I'm going mad', and he couldn't understand how I felt.

> My mother had made it obvious that she didn't want anything to do with bringing up her grandchildren. She wouldn't baby-sit, she wouldn't look after them during the day or anything. She'd got her kids off her hands and she wanted her freedom.

Her marital situation worsened, and she and her husband separated and eventually divorced:

> Things with my husband were getting very, very bad, and I said, 'Look, I've got to do something about this', I don't know whether it was him or just the situation but we ended up with a trial separation where he went to South Africa for a year and left me with the kids. So I went along to the local day nursery, and said, 'I'm a single parent, please can I put my kids in the nursery and can I get a job?' I managed to get a job as a clerical assistant, and that was great until he decided to come back from South Africa. He said they wouldn't give him a resident's permit while he was separated. So were we going to get back together again, or were we going to get divorced? and I said, 'I'm quite enjoying being on my own', the only problem was, by this time, the eldest lad was five, he was at school, and I was having problems with child-care during the holidays. So after a bit of argy-bargy, we decided that he would have custody of the kids and I would be on my own.

Leila did not mention the children again after this point. She went on to tell me that she formed a close relationship with another partner who was encouraging her to return to education. Unfortunately he died very suddenly, leaving her in very difficult financial circumstances.

> About this time I'd met this other feller, and he said, 'Well if you're stuck for somewhere to live, come and live with me', and we got a quite close relationship there. I think he was pushing me towards getting a University place then, but he died before anything came of it, and then of course I've got no money, no house, so it's a question of trying to get a better job, trying to find somewhere else to live. And then I was just sort of living from hand to mouth really, until Dan came along and moved in with me and then we got a bit of spare money. I did a TOPS course to do the computer programming and we've been doing OK ever since then.

For this student, there is intrinsic satisfaction in the course she is doing, but there is also a strong element of proving to herself that she has some academic ability. She went on to reinforce this point and also to tell me how much her confidence had grown since she started studying again:

> I feel more confident, I have got a brain ... that first day (at college) I felt terrible! Very self-conscious, no confidence at all, wondering a lot about what sort of people they were going to be on the course, whether they were all going to be really, really clever. Apart from learning a lot of, well I won't call it useless information ... it's proving to me that I can still do it, that my memory's not gone, though it takes me a bit longer to store it. I've remembered a lot of things that I learnt at school, it's rather surprised me how much of what I learnt 25 years ago is still there. I averaged 92 percent overall in the first lot of exams. I was pleased I'd come out top to be honest - relieved.

Leila had reached a point in her life where a number of factors, including her redundancy, had made her address her whole identity. Her return to education has served a number of purposes. She is clearly enjoying the course and finds considerable intrinsic satisfaction in studying - she makes this point quite clearly when she talks of the course being 'a bit of self-indulgence'. She also maintains that she has gained considerable confidence in both herself and her ability and although she hoped for a better job at the end of her course; this wasn't of primary importance, her major benefits are in the here and now.

Summary

These students then, met different major events in their lives which created a watershed and precipitated an examination of who and what they were. Of course, many of us have similar experiences as we get older, and may make some re-assessment of ourselves, but not all of us decide to come back into education. Why they chose education as opposed to other vehicles for changing their lives was not within the parameters of this research, but what is important are the links which the women make between their lives and their return to learning. For all the women, the links with education are in terms of identity, through a better job, a testing of ability, a fear of disability and the realisation of unfulfilled potential. For Heather, Deidre and Liz, education has been therapeutic, though not necessarily in the same way; it was something to occupy and stretch their mental capacity, albeit for different reasons. Deidre, Liz and Leila particularly talked of an increase in their confidence, which links them closely with the women in the next chapter.

5 Childhood experiences

Most of the traumatic experiences which the women reported have some roots in what happened in their childhood years and many of them reported a restrictive and controlling parent. For Gloria and Alison it was a father; as it had been with Leila in the previous chapter, but for Dilys, the problem was her mother. However, experiences were by no means restricted to life within a family and Vida, Aurora and Alison talked of wider social influences on their lives. Some of the students had later painful experiences too and Aurora and Alison particularly go on to talk about these. This chapter starts with Dilys's story of the considerable restrictions she experienced in her mainstream education.

Dilys

Dilys is 34, married with two children aged 12 and 9. She is studying at a local college on the second year of both a full-time secretarial course which is three full days a week and a part-time social studies and humanities course which is one day a week. She also works four evenings a week. I asked Dilys why she had not continued her education at sixteen:

> Because my parents didn't want me to get well educated, I know that sounds awful, but it's true. I was in the top form at school, and I got three O-Levels. Now my older sister got expelled from school, she was in a low grade, she hated school, she was always fighting and always at home, and so when I went to school, because I was in the top form, my friends were sort of - to my family - a little bit snobbish, so I couldn't take friends home and all this, and I never, ever got encouraged to go to school ...

Although she talks of her parents lacking interest in her education, she lays the blame primarily with her mother:

> My mam used to make me have time off school to clean the house ...
> And I were cooking the tea and all this, that's how it was, I just didn't get any support at all.

When Dilys was offered a place at a local college of further education, she was unable to take it because of family pressure:

> The deputy head advised me to go on a catering course at this college and I got on it and when they gave me the details, you'd got to pay something like £70 for a set of knives and I told my mum and my mum said, 'No chance, we're not buying them, get out of there and get a job' ... and so I got out there, got a job as a trainee manager at a supermarket and my mum just wanted that wage coming in, you know. She was working, and my dad was working, so looking back, she didn't need the money, and my uncle lived with us. I didn't get on with my uncle, so I didn't have a very good home life anyway.

Dilys told me that she never really questioned her home situation at the time, rather, she thought the problem lay with herself:

> There was four of us and I was different to the others. I always liked reading, I liked books ... but I always thought it was me that was weird. You don't know do you, you don't know until you're older, so I used to pretend that I didn't care about school and when my mum made me have time off, I thought, 'Well that's alright', because I wanted her to think I was like my sister, 'cos she got on with my sister and everything, but it didn't do me any good because even now we don't get on. I'm still classed as a bit of a snob and - but I'm not, I don't talk like a snob as you can hear me, but it's just that I'm different. I know what I want and I love to learn.

Despite their lack of support for Dilys's early education, her parents' attitude is apparently still important to her. Even now, her mother has a negative attitude towards her education, although she is changing and her father does ask her about her courses:

> Well when I first told my mam I was going back to college, her reaction was 'what are you doing that for?' She used to go out of the room when me dad used to ask me about it, 'cos me dad's always asked me, and he'd say, 'how're you going on at college?' and me mum'd say, 'Are you putting t'kettle on?' and she didn't want to know. I felt, well, she obviously doesn't want to know ... but now, she will ask me.

Although this student was very keen to talk to me and volunteered without any hesitation, she came late to the interview, her body language was defensive and she talked in a rapid non-stop fashion. I got the impression that there had been many more problems at home than she was willing to talk about. When I asked the question 'is it just things about your education that were a problem at home, or were there other things?' she responded only cursorily:

> There were other things as well, yeah, there were lots of other things, but education was one. I resent that they didn't support me and I know I shouldn't, but I do and I think it's sad that they didn't but I've got to just come to terms with the fact that we'll never really have a close, loving relationship, me and my mum and dad ...

I asked her whether she blamed herself for that. Her response indicates a poor self-image, and although this is changing, there are still problem areas for her:

> Oh I did, I always have done. I used to say, 'well it's got to be me, they can't be wrong because if my mum argues with anybody, if she falls out with anybody, everybody's got to follow suit, and when we fell out for fourteen months, it was only an argument between me and my ma, but my sisters didn't talk to me, nor my father, for fourteen months, they all disowned me ... it's just been a battle ...

Dilys's return to education has been the culmination of many years of waiting:

> I've always wanted to go back into education but it's always been evening classes and we've never had the money ... When I was nineteen I went away to work. I met my future husband, came back, married him and had a little boy straight away ... so I've waited all these years to go back, but I've dreamed about it more-or-less ever since I had my little boy, and realised that was it, once I'd had my little boy, I thought, 'God, this is it, there's no more opportunity, I can't just go out there and do it, I've got him to think about now all the time', and it hit like a ton of bricks, and ever since then I've always thought, you know, one day I will ...

Dilys makes an interesting point here about her realisation of the enormity of her restrictions and responsibilities with the birth of her son. She was very aware at this time in her life that her caring responsibilities would curtail her ambitions, at least for the foreseeable future, but she did not resent this responsibility. This reflects the acceptance by the majority of the women of their responsibilities for their children, even though they may reject an identity totally located within the home. Dilys goes on to talk about her determination to encourage her children towards the education she felt she never had:

... but if I don't, my kids will. I've really encouraged them, I don't push them, I don't believe in pushing anybody ...

This student has made a number of what she considers to be very personal gains from education - one is her increase in confidence, which she linked with a more acceptable self-image:

When I came on the first day I was nervous as hell and I thought, 'God, what am I doing this for?' I was so scared, and I kept thinking, 'you're going to show yourself up, they're going to ask you all these things, they're going to talk about all these words that you don't know what they're talking about, and they're going to be all these posh people .'... But when I got talking to them, I felt like they're only like me ... It's made a big difference in me, it's given me a lot more confidence, it's shown me what opportunities there are out there.

Well, I see myself as much more confident, much happier about myself, I've had such a troubled childhood that it really bothered me, but coming back here, talking to people, I mean, ... we're all women, we're all about my age and we talk about everything and it really does you good. And it's nice, it's just nice to be gaining qualifications and bettering yourself and I just feel a lot happier about myself.

I'm proud of myself, to be honest, I'm very proud of myself ... It's made me value me a lot I think, my friends, my time, my work, my job, you know. It's made me see myself a lot differently, and I'm a lot happier about myself. A lot more relaxed, and I feel as if I've got a lot more to give to my kids, you know.

Another gain is her second chance at opportunities she felt were denied in her youth:

For me, it was reliving a childhood that I feel I lost. I mean, I don't want to make it sound like sob-story, but it is, it really has been for me and my support has been Bob (her husband), and he's been the parent that I didn't have. So I feel lucky that I've got this opportunity. I've had it and it's been lovely.

Finally, at least some independence from the influence of her extended family:

Doing this for me is a way of breaking away. I can be even more independent from them ... and having that support from Bob means he's coming with me ... It's been the making of me, it really has.

Clearly, the qualifications which Dilys is gaining are important to her, but she is gaining in many other ways from education. She has not been successful this year in her application to the two local universities but she sees this as a temporary setback in a learning career she has long waited for. It seems to me that there have been major benefits for Dilys in shaping and changing some aspects of her identity. Firstly, the more positive self-image which she has acquired since being at college has enabled her gradual independence from the negative influence of her extended family. Secondly, she has gained a great deal of confidence, and thirdly, she is accomplishing a long-held desire to fulfil her potential and prove her ability.

The support which Dilys has had from her husband, links her with the next student, Alison, though unlike Dilys, it was her father and not her mother who was the controlling factor in her early years.

Alison

Alison told me that her father was manipulative and controlling during her childhood and teen years. She is currently a full-time student on a social science access course at a local college, with offers of places in higher education. Aged 34, she is married and living with her partner and three children aged 14, 9 and 5.

Alison was the only girl of six children and her relationship with her father had been difficult. She described fairly frequent violence in the house, between her parents and between her father and her brothers. Money was always short because of her father's gambling habit (although she did not realise this was the problem until much later):

> ... from being fourteen when I first did my paper round, I ended up at loggerheads with my dad because his family tradition was that when you started work you came home and you put the money on the table, the parents took what they wanted and gave back what bit they thought you were entitled to. After doing my first week's paper round he asked for me to give him all the money, and I had an argument with him, saying, 'No, I've worked for it, I'm keeping it'. After that it was six months out of every year we just never spoke to each other. Although I loved him very much we just disagreed on so much. From being about fourteen to twenty one our relationship was appalling - really bad.

She goes on to describe her father's manipulation of her life:

> My ambition on leaving school was to go into the police force but that managed to get completely messed up with the help of my dad ...

I was going out with a gypsy ... he phoned up the Chief Inspector and told him I was a dishonest deceitful daughter - and not to touch me with a barge pole. So I went into a two-bit job for two years - just as a telephonist/ receptionist - which my dad got me ... very much a manipulator.

After moving away from home and into a flat in the same area as her parents, she then went to work in a seaside resort, but each time her father put pressure on her to return:

... my dad was phoning me up telling me that my mother was ill - all a pack of lies - but enough to put the pressure on me to pack up and come home ... then ... telling me how ill he was with his heart attacks - and they were all fakes.

I just kept thinking he was doing it for my interests - he cared about me and wanted me home where I was safe but when I was at home he was terrible. If I went out at night, he'd be waiting at the top of the street - ready to drag out whoever was in the car, taxi or whatever I came home in ... He really was impossible - his violent mood swings were terrible.

The following year whilst working in London, she became very ill with pneumonia and returned home. Although she was taking contraceptives, the doctor did not warn her that their effectiveness was reduced by antibiotics and she became pregnant. She discovered that her 'boyfriend' - the father of the child - was actually engaged to someone else. When she told her own father of the pregnancy, his response was very negative:

I'd told my mum and she was fine about it, no problems there, and he went up the wall. And for the whole of the eight months he never spoke to me, not two words, at all. It was just terrible 'cos he just shut me out completely the whole time ...

Up to being eight months pregnant, Alison slept on the settee in the two-bedroomed house, with a brother and her parents occupying the two bedrooms. The only time her father did communicate with her was when she physically intervened in family violence:

When anyone came in drunk or arguing or something like that and I would get up and get in between them, and he would just simply say, 'If anything happens to that baby I'll swing for you'.

Her father's behaviour gave Alison a very clear negative message - she wasn't important, but the baby was. Her poor self-image, which she talks about later, was further reinforced after the baby was born:

> But having said that, the minute she was born - he was there ... he idolised her ... at night when she was crying he'd be the first one in with a bottle.

Alison met her husband the following year. They married the year after and she had two more children. She told me that her husband has been very supportive:

> He could see right through my dad and he wouldn't let anybody manipulate me, so on that he was very good for me. And he's also done a great deal to build up my confidence, teach me how capable I am. He's just taught me so much, you know, it's like a different world. And in many ways, the influence he has on me is what I wish my father would have had at sixteen ...

Alison and her husband have done voluntary work with young people for about 10 years. When I asked her why she had gone back into education she told me:

> I'd like to go into teaching and I'd like to become a special needs teacher because during the course of the youth work, I was staggered by how many children couldn't read at the age of fourteen, fifteen and I just felt that I could make a difference. I'm sure I can make a difference and that's why I want to go back.

She told me that this job would be an extension of her voluntary work and went on to say that her one regret about being on the course is her lack of time for neighbours and friends and their problems:

> My door was always open and I would have a constant stream of visitors - usually people with problems. Somebody perhaps just wanting someone to talk to - of all ages - and I think they're the losers this year. Nobody can find me any more, I'm just never here. And there are times when I'm questioning myself, saying 'Well have I done the right thing here?' because it was something I enjoyed doing. I honestly don't know.

She does however recognise that having a constant ear for others' problems is reflective of a need in herself to establish a positive identity. Alison's father died recently and she has been having counselling to help her sort out her conflicting feelings:

When I was talking to this lady counsellor about my dad, one thing she'd said was the fact that I felt I'd got to be liked by everybody. And I think that's very true.

You feel everyone's got to like you and you're constantly doing things I think, because you're not happy with who you are. I think it's got a lot to do with proving yourself and feeling the need to prove yourself. And although it came naturally to me, when you look behind it and find out why, it's usually because of your insecurities.

Her voluntary work and her husband's support have given Alison a boost to her confidence, but she is still looking for the confidence which comes from proving to herself that she has academic ability:

Personally, I'll say one thing the course has done, is I feel it's given me a great deal more confidence in my abilities. It's made me realise so much - I had such a low opinion - I'd got a very low opinion of what I was capable of doing. I'd been led to believe that it was going to be really hard and I'd never make it, and the family would suffer ...

Alison also expressed a need for a different identity from that which is located in her domestic role:

I know there's a point where the family's got to come first, but I also feel that if you're mentally frustrated you're no good to anybody. And, I just feel I was beginning to get very bored at home not knowing what to do next. I'm not the type of person that enjoys cleaning up all the time. I just needed to do something else and this has stretched me a great deal and I've just learned so much about so many things, I was just really glad.

The major benefit which this student has gained from education though is linked with self-worth and identity. She expressed the conflict she feels between her past and present lives:

My husband was a finance director. When he was in his last job, the people there were typical, I would say, finance directors' wives that thought they were really something, and I'd never felt like that. I've never felt good enough to be a finance director's wife! I always felt beneath everybody and yet, at the same time, because I live in a poor background area, because Christian's a finance director and has a good job and a good car, people still look up at me. I felt torn between the two and not felt that I knew where I belonged.

Within college, she feels she is able to define her own identity and is not constrained by the labels she feels have been attached. She talks of more independence and control over her life:

> While I've been on the course, because I've been mixing with people from all different backgrounds, I've felt very comfortable. I can relate to people again at an equal level. They've not looked up at me and seen me as a finance director's wife, they've just seen me. I don't feel I've been labelled - whereas before I felt I was labelled. You know? I was either Mrs ... the finance director's wife, or Alison, the unmarried mother. Because I'm still in the same area that all this has happened to me - because my parents just live two bus stops away - I've always felt I've had this label attached to me and I wanted to get away from it. I feel I've been able to do that this last year. I don't feel I've got any labels hanging over me at the moment. I feel a lot more independent.

Alison went on to talk about her feelings when she became pregnant, and the negative influence it had on her identity. She told me her return to education was definitely something for herself:

> I was so disappointed with myself becoming an unmarried mother - it was one thing I would never, ever wish on a child. You can tell a lie and your lies will not get caught out, but you get pregnant and it grows in front on you for eight, nine months and it's getting bigger and heavier all the time. And you feel weighed down by that, and that burden, I found, very hard to get rid of even when I got married. I'm sure it's affected me, you know, the way I've felt about myself ... I've had this really, really poor self image ...

> Definitely something personal. I wanted to prove to people that I could do it. I wanted to prove that I had got stickability. That I had got some worth. It's given me something positive.

Alison's relationship with her father and her pregnancy have had a major impact on her life and the way she sees herself. Her return to education is serving many purposes. Firstly, she has more control over defining her own identity. Secondly, she talks of independence, and by this I think she means freedom from the labels which have been attached, rather than economic freedom. Thirdly, she is proving her ability, both to herself and to others. Finally, the course itself is helping to build a positive self-image and is also the first step to paid employment in a job which she feels will give her some worth, both in her own and in others' eyes.

I asked this student what had been the main issue for her this year Her response, I think, puts into a nutshell the psychological benefit for Alison of her return to education:

> The main issue? For myself, I think getting rid of little skeletons in the cupboard ... the course has helped. I wouldn't have done it without being on the course.

The next student, Gloria, also talked of a manipulating and controlling father, albeit like Alison, with hindsight, but his control over her life took a different form.

Gloria

Gloria's determination to return to education, like Dilys's had its roots in her childhood. She is 38, married with two children aged 11 and 9. She is a student on the foundation year of a four-year degree in science. The course is franchised out to a local college from one of the universities in the area and attracts a mandatory grant. Gloria's father was the main influence on her mainstream education in two ways. Firstly, his job took the family around the country:

> Gloria: We moved around an awful lot, I went to eleven different schools and up to the age of eighteen I moved twenty two times. It was my father's job. He was in the forces to start off with and then he became area manager of a building society. Every time you settled down into something we were whisked off somewhere else. When I was doing my O levels, say for example in geography, I did a year of geography in Grimsby and then we moved to Derby and they'd started the other way round - so I started geography in Derby what I'd just done in Grimsby. It wears you down 'cos you're just sort of fighting against it. In the end I just thought, 'Right, well I might as well wait. An opportunity will surely present itself'.

Secondly, it was also her father's attitude which affected her. I asked Gloria whether her parents had been interested in her education. Her response reflects firstly the apparent dominance of her father in the family:

> No, not particularly. My mum was too busy pandering to the whims of my dad and my dad was too busy doing what he wanted to do, to benefit himself, which sounds all very bitter and twisted but it's not like that, it's just being realistic. No, he was more interested in his own needs - like a lot of men are at that age I think ...

and secondly her perception of his attitude generally towards women:

My dad ... he's a mysogynist. He was contemptuous of women and expected women to be barefoot, pregnant and at the kitchen sink most of the time. Any hint of education or intelligence was just squashed. You know - you can't have women with brains, they're not there for that. He's actually admitted he doesn't like women being educated. I sat and had a bottle of whiskey with him once and he said one of the reasons why we moved around as much as we did was because he didn't want me and Sarah, particularly, to be educated. That's an effort for me - a horrible thing to have to take. I know people have to put up with a lot worse, but educationally, it's rotten isn't it?

Like Dilys, Gloria felt that she had been deprived of her educational opportunities at the conventional age and had always wanted to return to formal learning. Coupled with this was the realisation that her children were becoming independent and this made her examine her own situation. In addition, she did not wish to return to the psychiatric nursing she had done prior to the birth of her children, because she had become disillusioned with the nursing profession. She recognised this period as a crucial time in her life:

I missed out on an education when I was younger really. Then when the kids were getting older I was thinking, 'well I want to do something'. I don't want to be sort of left at home thinking that my kids have gone off doing what they want to do, my husband's doing what he wants to do. It's a time when you think 'well, what am I going to do with the rest of my life?' They're big thoughts aren't they? And you have to make such big decisions. So I thought, 'right this is the ideal time to get myself started doing something that I want to do'. I wanted to go to college and the opportunity presented itself.

Gloria is looking for an identity outside the domestic sphere. I asked why she had chosen the science foundation course. She has an ambivalent attitude towards her subjects, but lays the blame for this firmly at the door of gendered education in her youth:

I've always had problems with maths, always had problems with it. I was frightened to death of it and yet I liked it. I liked physics but I was useless at it. Chemistry? I was a bit better at chemistry and I was very good at biology. And I thought I really like these subjects, but being a female and the age I was when I was younger at school women weren't encouraged to do science - unless you were absolutely brilliant - you were encouraged to go into domestic science as it was called then ... and then leave school and have babies or whatever ... So that interest has always been squashed and I just thought, right I can go and do it now if I want to.

Gloria told me that her main motivation was interest, but she acknowledges a need to reject the power that her father has had in defining her identity:

Mostly the motivation, believe it or not, is because I want to do it because I'm interested. But what makes me do it is probably, you know, 'I'm going to show him (her father)'. We have heated battles - or we have had. Even now if I 'phone him up and tell him, what I'm doing, he says he's, sort of, pleased but I know that it's irritating him to death.

Gloria's father seems to have been a powerful negative force in her past. She challenges not only her father's power, but also what she sees as the power of men generally, to have control over women's identity:

The biggest thing for me is male attitudes and I know where that comes from - but I see it all around me as well. What right do they have, you know, to think they're better than us? ... That's why, for me, their definition of masculinity is questionable isn't it? And they never stop to question it because what makes them feel macho and masculine is by undermining those who they consider to be weaker than themselves - which is women and, unfortunately, children as well. Even at 38 it still makes me mad.

The whole interview was underpinned with a general distaste for sexism and a cynical recognition of its effect in all areas of her life, both past and present:

I think one of the worst things I've come across is when people find out that I've come to college and it's 'what are you playing at now?' You know, this kind of attitude and 'don't you think you should be at home looking after your children?' - this kind of thing, which really makes me angry.

Just talking to people in a pub or even family sometimes - these really nice people that you love and they come out with things like that and you think, 'well, because I want to do something with myself'. Some people resent it don't they? When you try and prove your ability and seem to achieve - they don't like it. Sometimes people make you feel you're apologising for what you're doing.

Proving her ability has been quite important for Gloria:

I've proved to myself that I can achieve academically. And that's always been a big thing for me because it's always been squashed, as I said before. It's not been against all odds because I think people are in far worse situations than I am, but for me personally, it's proved a lot.

Achievement per se is important for this student, but she also wants to achieve a degree which will give her a better job. She wanted to teach, but felt that this was not a realistic option:

What's the point of me going in for a B.Ed when eventually it's going to become obsolete when they bring this mum's army in? There's no point in me, at forty three - that's when I'll finish - having a degree that is going to be neither use nor ornament - it's just like a waste of all the time I've spent. Well it's not a waste, 'cos it means you've done something, it's an achievement but I won't be able to do a great deal with it. And it's important that I can do something with it at forty three. So I'm going to do Biomedical Sciences.

Gloria, like Dilys, is fulfilling a long-held desire to achieve her potential and to prove her ability. She is another student who seems to have reached a watershed in her life, where her children are becoming independent and she is looking for an identity outside the home. She is also resisting her father's definition of her self and what she sees as sexist attitudes generally. Her return to education, and particularly her choice of course, is helping her to meet these needs and also to define and thus to have some power and control over her identity.

Gloria's fragmented early education and movement from school to school, links her with Vida, who had also had a somewhat chequered education, moving around several times during her school years because of her father's occupation.

Vida

Vida is 37, married, with three children. She is in the second year of a social science dual honours degree at a local university. Her early education was very fragmented, largely due to her father's occupation in the forces. Most of her secondary education was in the UK, where she and her sister and brother experienced some cultural racism because her mother was German. She told me that she was less affected by this than her siblings were, but then contradicts this somewhat:

My mother took my brother to the primary school and the stupid teacher said 'we've got a little German boy here'. Well he never lived it down. He was a nazi and all the rest of it, but you know what kids are like - really cruel. We always got that over here but you get used to it. We went back over to Germany and it was great being back with people like yourself. I always felt more comfortable in the army schools because they were people like you and there is a difference and they understood.

She dealt with the racism and constant moving by making herself popular in two ways, firstly by being good at sport:

I would find out where the sports room was, I knew I was good at it, but yes it was a conscious effort ...

and secondly by being one of the crowd:

We went to Leeds and we were there for 18 months so I was about 13 or 14 while I was there and I went off the rails a bit ... I don't know whether I would have done that anyway or what but ...

Vida's experiences in this school were not like her previous ones and she was concerned that she might be seen as 'different' from the others:

I can remember leaning out of this window at school and talking about VD and me just knowing I didn't know what VD was and I'm thinking 'God don't let them ask me a question' because I didn't know and I would have been so embarrassed and the other thing was that the first day at that school there was a lot of this lads pulling the girls clothes off - that kind of thing. It wasn't attempted rape or anything like that but I can remember being extremely upset about it and I can remember this girl saying 'don't worry about it, it always happens, it's always one of our turns, they all sort of mess about - see what bra you're wearing and all this kind of thing'.

Vida's group membership led her into early sexual adventures. When this came to light, she feels she was treated very badly as a female, with her personal identity violated by adults who had control over her:

There was one lad had a party - his parents had gone to Majorca. Big party, loads of cider - people ended up in bed with each other. There were kids younger than me and one girl, her parents called her bluff and accused her. She gave the whole game away for everybody and the police called round the house. That was awful, they took my passport away - kept coming back - had to write a statement. It was a really horrible experience and the girls were really dragged through it and had to go for a virginity test. I can remember the bloke who did the internal with my mother there who was absolutely in tears and all the rest of it because I'd failed it. The whole school knew about it. There was this ink we couldn't get off the passport and it was quite horrible. All the lads were gathered down the police station and sort of warned keep it tucked in until they were 16 but the girls were really dragged through it.

It was over the holiday time and I can remember going back and being really embarrassed and just knowing that the teachers knew because the school had been informed. It didn't actually hit the papers or go to court in the end but we were threatened with all of that but it was a big thing, not so much for me but for my parents.

She speculates on whether 'going off the rails' was simply to be one of a crowd and reflected her need for a group identity:

Whether that would have happened anyway, because maybe I'm just that kind of person or whether it was all linked up to moving schools and all this settling and wanting to be accepted doing what every one else is doing because it was that kind of school because they were all very worldly wise and I wasn't and I sort of jumped off a cliff to join them. I think really so.

At this point she talks of her father's violence and although she appears to play it down, she speculates on her resistance to his control:

I was just so upset because my dad was always a bit handy with undoing his belt and giving us a good ... I've had bruises across my backside and my legs. If lads came they had to wait by the gate, they weren't allowed up to the door - very strict on that count so perhaps that had some encouragement in me doing that ... I continued to be off the rails a little bit but then I sat for my O-levels and I got five, then started A-levels and decided that I wanted to be a nurse. I can remember when I told my dad across the table I was packing it in and he just slapped me across my face once and then he said you're staying and I said I'm not. I stuck to my guns.

Vida's early school and home life were fragmented and her experiences painful. It is interesting that she constantly tried to explain her behaviour as she was talking to me. She qualified as a nurse, and after her marriage and three children, continued to work on a part-time basis. However, she was becoming increasingly frustrated and disillusioned with nursing because of the lack of promised training opportunities. She also talked about the competing demands which had been made on her by her roles in the public world of work and in the private world of her roles as wife, mother and housewife:

They were very much into nurse education and they promised me that I could go on some courses, but this just wasn't coming ...

I thought 'sod it you (nursing) are not the miracle I want'. I've given a lot of my life to nursing and midwifery and worked hard ... partly, the nursing - you're giving something of yourself all the time. If it's not to your patients, it's to your children; it's to your husband. They're all competing for what you can give them ... I'm going to do something for me now.

Looking for some mental stimulation, Vida returned to education, initially part-time, then full-time on an access course. She progressed from the access course to a local university, and this last sentence mirrors what is threaded through her story from this point on. There are clear statements that her return to education, at all levels, is for herself, and there is some intrinsic satisfaction in the actual learning process:

I wanted to do something that stimulated me. I felt like I'd had my head in a nappy bucket for years, nursing had gone off the boil and I wanted to do something that I found interesting you know and maybe I'd do better at a degree if I just did single honours, but I quite enjoy the dual. It might mean getting not so good a degree but I'll enjoy the combination of the both and I think you have to look at what you're enjoying as well.

This university thing is something for me ... it was mine ... this was giving **me** something.

Vida's university education is helping her to prove her ability - not only to her husband and his family, but also to herself. She links this need with her earlier experiences at school:

I wanted to prove to myself I could get to university because my husband had been and all his brothers and sisters had been. I can remember once 'daddy cleverer than mummy because he goes to work' that kind of thing and I thought 'sod that he isn't'.

I wanted to prove to myself and other people that I could do it and I believed that I could. There's definitely a driving force somewhere, I don't know what it is. A lot of it might stem back to all this school trauma thing that I went through.

Vida expressed a need for independence and a separate identity from that located in her marital role:

The other thing was that I knew once I started that although I would discuss things with Jeremy - things we studied or whatever, I wanted this just to be for me. I didn't want him to know my friends down there either, which he found pretty strange, but I know that women, and it happened with me, you end up giving up a lot of your friends and taking on your husband's friends.

Overt resistance to her partner's and others' control emerged and this began to cause considerable conflict with her husband:

I think I started fighting for what I wanted a bit more. I started not wanting Jeremy. I wanted to go out on my own with my friends and I had to fight for one night out a week. Once I had one, I wanted two nights out. As far as I was concerned that rounded off the whole university thing. So fights and arguments about going out was just awful and once or twice Jeremy insisted on coming with me which really annoyed me and we had some right stand-ups. Then I got involved with somebody that I ought not to have done.

Vida's husband found out about the affair and began to put financial and emotional pressure on her. She attained some independence by moving out of the marital home during the exam period, but this was not satisfactory and seemed to increase her problems:

I decided I was going to move out because I just couldn't cope with the hassle and it wasn't doing the kids any good either - they started to see us arguing and that's one thing I really didn't want them to do. It started affecting my work and I moved out to study. Of course I could go out when I wanted to, so I went out with my friends and actually did quite a lot of drinking and getting drunk, really went off the rails ...

The situation with her husband deteriorated and as he attempted more control, she became increasingly resistant to it, particularly when her father became involved:

I insisted on staying out for the full six weeks and then things started getting horrible. Then he got a solicitor without telling me - he was going to get the car back and stop the money. So I went to see a solicitor, then I had a major row with my dad. My dad was saying things to Jeremy like 'you were far too soft with her, you should never have let her go to university, you should never have let her have a car'.

Vida returned home at the end of the six weeks, but her heightened perception of her husband's attempts to control her led to a further deterioration in their relationship. She became increasingly resentful of this control and the way her identity had been defined thus far, though she does acknowledge that she had been happy to go along with this:

> I resented it and that was partly why I went of the rails a bit ... this control thing which I did start feeling or suddenly realised. It was partly of my making because I slotted into a situation that I didn't realise was happening and it obviously served my purpose, Jeremy's purpose, all the rest of it, at the time. I don't want to paint him out to be the worst person ever and he's very considerate in a lot of ways and yet when I looked back on certain things, he made decisions about things. His decision would be the one that was taken in the end and I started resenting it ...

She challenged her husband's definition of the situation and rejected her domestic (though not her mothering) identity:

> He says we've always had an equal relationship and I've always been able to voice what I want and I said 'no I haven't because obviously that's what I'm doing now and its not going down very well. I want my own friends, my own little corner but it doesn't suit any more so sod it no, I'm sorry I've got an essay to write, I'm not ironing shirts - you're as capable of ironing as I am. I'm doing a full time course now which in my opinion is equivalent to your full time work, it might not be bringing any money but then again you're earning enough for both of us and I helped you earn that in the first place'. I got to being very articulate in my arguments and he didn't like that.

Vida denies her husband's assertion that she has changed:

> He said 'you've changed'. I said 'I don't think I have changed, I think it's been there all the time. It's been sort of suppressed and now I've found myself in an environment where I can express myself and that's spilled over to home and you don't like it ... well, if you don't like it, you can just lump it'.

Returning to education, and going to university in particular, appears to have created a watershed in Vida's life - a time which is affecting her whole sense of herself. Her existing situation appears to be traumatic. There is considerable turmoil in her life, in terms of her relationships and her identity, but she is determined not to give up her education, nor her newly found independence. She makes clear links between her past, her education and her current difficult situation. She argues that it is not a new

Vida, rather an existing aspect of her identity which she knew was there, but is only now emerging. As she says:

> I think gradually it has been a metamorphosis of me.

Like Vida and Gloria, Aurora, whose story is the final one in the chapter, had a fragmented early education, though for very different reasons. The cultural racism which Aurora told me she experienced appears to have had a much more profound effect on her life.

Aurora

Aurora is 22, divorced and living alone with a 2 year old daughter. She is also enrolled at a local college on the foundation year of a 4-year science degree. She told me that her first painful experiences were at school, which resulted in her changing schools frequently, attending sporadically:

> Well originally when I was at school, I was racially abused. This sounds hard because I know I'm white, but my mother was German and there was a boy at school and he knew about this and he took it into the comprehensive school - and there was a lot of trouble because of the forty years of war celebrations, forty years since war had begun. And I got school phobia as it was, and went to several comprehensive schools and the last one I went to, I went back a year. It sort of put me off school. Took a lot of will power to get back into school and then I missed another year there, finally got back to school, did my GCSE's and I thought 'that's it, I've had enough'.

I asked how her parents handled the racial abuse:

> I can't really go into it 'cos er, the racial view wasn't just directed at me it was directed at my brother - he went back a year when he changed schools when he was being abused - and then this, one guy sort of messed up the first year of his A levels ... This is really complicated but to cut a long story short, there's certain top politicals in Austen who erm, actually decided to erm, start action against my family. Particularly ... against my father and they actually decided that they were going to cause my mum to have a nervous breakdown - and it killed her ... She died when I was fourteen.

At this point Aurora became quite distressed, and I switched off the tape and reassured her that she didn't have to talk about anything which she found too distressing. She told me she would be alright providing she didn't go into too much detail. She moved from this topic and went on to tell me that she had left school and worked in insurance. She had become pregnant at nineteen and brought her planned marriage forward. Her husband's violence, not apparent prior to their marriage, emerged almost immediately:

> I was working for a while, then I got married. I had a daughter and I actually had to leave my husband because there was abuse ... Well, not openly at my daughter all the time ... I went in a refuge for a fortnight. Then the council got me a flat.

> The minute we got married he completely changed. It was like Jekyll and Hyde. It became very frightening - the doctor actually said afterwards that, well from the description of what I gave him it sounded like he was a paranoid schizophrenic. Apparently they're very good at hiding what they're like. But also, it wasn't just him it was his parents attitude to it all. I think the strain was really from them. His family was actually encouraging the lying. It was my hardest thing to believe.

> They had another granddaughter who was illegitimate, and they just pandered to her. They didn't want her to just walk out and leave with the kid. They didn't have any rights as far as she was concerned, whereas with me, I was married, they'd got a hold on me, I was stuck then. They could do what they liked to me and I'd have to put up with it. So they just tortured me. And, well they tried taking me to court for contact with my daughter but they didn't get anywhere. I don't have anything to do with them ...

Aurora returned to education because she was bored at home, and the course was 'a chance to try something new'. Her father looks after her daughter, and they seem to have a mutual support system. She tends not to get too friendly with the other students, but recognises that this is probably because of her past experiences:

> I know some of them are quite good and I'm friendly with them, but they support each other more than anything. I certainly keep myself going ... I've always been a bit of a loner. I get on with everybody, but I'm not friends with everybody, I don't get too pally. I suppose that's partly because of the way I've been treated. I don't like to get too close to people. I think I've learned to put a front on ... I've had to, to survive ... it's all my experiences that have made me the way I am ... I'm a real fighter, which I think is the reason I keep going ...

She told me that her main aim from the course is independence through a well-paid job, though she does not have a specific career plan:

> ... to get a degree and then get a nice job and get lots of money. Well, I'm so used to managing on such little money that if I got a job that

did pay a lot of money I'd probably have a lot of money saved up in the bank. It's a form of security isn't it? I know there's certain areas that I can go into, like, spaces in research, I don't know exactly what, it's very, sort of, general at the moment, what I'd like to do. I don't want to remain on social security benefits for ever, paying the bills and left with nothing.

This student told me that the biggest gain from the course this year was confidence, but she is also beginning to recognise her academic ability:

The thing at the back of my mind, is can I really do this? Am I good enough? You know? I did OK in the last semester - I did two chemistry exams and got 92 percent for both of them and 93 percent in biology. The one I didn't do so well on was the maths. I got 78 percent in maths ... so I feel a bit more confident about the next lot of exams coming up next month.

There are many issues which this student is working through, a few of which are being addressed in her return to education. During the whole interview, her body language was very protective. Her arms were folded, her legs crossed and she was sitting right back in the corner of her chair. She did relax a little as we talked, but frequently her answers to my questions were minimal, especially when getting close to personal feelings. Once the tape had been switched off, she told me that her confidence had been badly damaged by her early experiences and was further affected by her marriage, but she was determined 'to do something with my life'. For Aurora, education certainly seems to be acting as a vehicle for independence and an improved self-image.

Summary

Aurora's need to have some control over her life reflects one of the most powerful factors in all the women's narratives. All of them talked of different events in their childhood which had a major influence on their lives and had affected their self-perception in some way. There was a common rejection of, or a need to modify, the way in which some part of their identity has been defined, either by their family, past or present, or by others in society. This was reflected in a desire to redefine these parts of their identity for themselves. In addition, for those students with household and caring responsibilities, there was a need for something outside of their domestic role - this was particularly strong for Vida and Gloria.

The women were gaining much more from their return to education than the qualifications from the course on which they were enrolled. A common factor for all women, was a need to prove, both to themselves and to others, that they had academic ability - something which for many of them, had been thwarted in their childhood. For Dilys and Gloria particularly, a return to education was a long-awaited opportunity to achieve something they felt they had been denied.

Another common thread was a strong desire for independence. This is not generally financial independence, although this was mentioned. Rather, it was personal independence - the need to be seen as individuals in their own right, with greater control over their lives than they have had hitherto.

Important too, was the need for a positive self-image. It is not just the way others see them which is important to the women returners, but also the way they see themselves. This is linked with the growing confidence which many women reported. For most of the students, this need for a different self-image appeared to coincide with a particular stage in their lives, or particular events which made them reassess themselves and their identities and then prompted a consideration of a return to education.

These mature students were grouped together because they reported painful experiences in their childhood which have had some effect on the rest of their lives. Most of these experiences were located within the family, but there were powerful social influences at work too, just as there were with the students in the next chapter, where unplanned pregnancies led them into difficult and restrictive relationships.

6 Unplanned pregnancies, life course and a return to education

Whereas the women in the previous chapter had talked of painful experiences in their early childhood, for Claire, Bryony, Frances and Jenny, it was the circumstances surrounding unplanned pregnancies which led them into controlling restrictive relationships. Again, what each of the women has to say is unique and the students have made very different links between their experiences and their return to education. Claire for example, is looking for some independence in the male dominated world of car maintenance. Bryony and Frances express a need for independence which is linked with their resistance to their partner's desire to locate them primarily within the home. The chapter ends with Jenny's story in which she describes not only the restrictions within her marital relationship, but also those of the neighbourhood in which she lives. All the students link education and identity through talk of confidence and proving their ability which is not only a common factor within the group, it also links them with students in previous chapters.

Claire

Claire is 31, divorced with 2 children. As well as running her own dress-making business, based on an industrial estate, she is a full-time student on a women's motor vehicle course at a local college. She mentioned little about her early family life, although it does not seem to have been particularly happy. Her difficulties appeared to start when she became pregnant and was married, at sixteen. However, it was not the children, but her relationship with her husband which was the problem:

> Claire: I left school at sixteen, straight after my O levels. I had my first baby at sixteen and I left school and then went straight into the marriage and had two children. I was sixteen and eighteen when I had my children, but I was quite maternal at that age actually. I couldn't cope with it now, but when they were younger, I was quite happy to look after them at home. But I was more restricted by my

husband. You know, he was really jealous so I didn't socialise or do anything. I lost all my friends ...

He left when I was eighteen so since then I've just been on my own. Well, I threw him out actually. Make no bones about it. He was violent and I wasn't prepared to put up with it. I didn't see that he was likely to get any better so - I've been on my own since then. So basically I didn't do anything at all for fourteen years, I've just stared at the walls.

After this point, Claire did not discuss the violence further, but when the tape was switched off, she told me that her husband had been quite violent. She had a nervous breakdown after he left and spent two years 'drugged up to the teeth' just lying on the settee either asleep or just looking at the walls, with 'the kids running round me'. Her benefit from education is two-fold. She has always been interested in motor mechanics, but it is also a topic which can serve her fierce desire for independence:

I just wanted to learn about motor vehicles. I've always wanted to learn about them, and well last year, actually, was the first time that I heard about the course. It's not as a career move. It's just to satisfy my own curiosity and interests. If I'm interested in something then I want to learn about it. I'll probably do the exams, well I will do the exam at the end. I may be interested in taking it up for a year or two, but not as a sort of full time occupation. Just to basically keep my own car going without having to pay someone else to do it, and fetch somebody else round every time something conks out. It's saved me a lot already and it galls me to have to ask anybody to fix it 'cos I don't know how. I like to know how to do everything just about.

Janet: So there's a streak of independence in you there, is there?

More than a streak I'd think, yes. I don't like to have to rely on anybody at all. Well I've nobody to run to - so it's taking it to a garage and I'm not happy about that, so - I've never had anybody looking after me so I've always had to get on and do it myself. You can't rely on people so how can you depend on them?

She gets a great deal of intrinsic satisfaction from the course, which is linked largely with her interest and the fact that it is giving her independence:

The course is brilliant really 'cos everybody gets on really well, I think everybody enjoys it because we don't take it as seriously as the boys even though we may be serious about what we're doing ... to learn it's fun for us.

I suppose they're expected to follow it up as a career ... you know, work and this sort of thing. We're doing it - even if we would like to follow it on and make a career out of it - we're doing it because we're interested in it. I mean, if you're not interested, if a woman isn't interested in motor vehicle mechanics she's not going to come on a course, you know, not just to earn a living, they'll find other ways of doing it - go and get a cleaning job or something if you need to earn a few pounds. So it's, yes, it's fun. I would be really upset if there was any reason why I had to give it up.

Claire also mentioned a change in herself which she links with her growing confidence. I asked her if she thought she had changed since coming on the course:

I'm very shy ... I'm enjoying myself more. It really is the only time I see anybody, you know, I occasionally see somebody in the corridor at work, but to talk to and to have a laugh with it's the only time I see anyone, so, yes I would say that I've become a bit more outgoing - and I've been more confident ...

Claire's return to education and her enjoyment of the course is linked in with her fierce desire for independence and control over her own life, but also, it has given her an increase in confidence and certainly a more positive self-image.

My interview with Claire was quite difficult. She was quiet with closed body language. I found it difficult to get her to talk freely - most of her answers were short and some were quite cynical. She told me that generally she didn't talk seriously to anyone because 'people mostly don't listen and why waste your breath?' As the interview went on, she relaxed a little, but gentle attempts at probing for more information were not successful.

Bryony

Bryony is the second of this group of students who were pregnant in their teens before marriage. She is 46, married with three children, two of whom are away from home. She is studying on a full-time science access course at a local college which will give her an acceptable entry qualification into higher education. She told me that she thought she had wasted her early education, particularly her 11+ opportunity:

Bryony: I think I've had quite a poor education - I went to a church school and I took my eleven plus and failed it deliberately. I've only told about two people that in my life because I feel so ashamed. I wanted to stay with my friends, and I knew my friends wouldn't get there. But I actually didn't find it too bad so I put the wrong answers down. I did tell my mother at the time in case I got found out. So then I went to a school on the east side of Austen, which was a poor school. I used to do the minimum work, really, to get me through, but I didn't get any encouragement from home. They didn't really mind whether I did well or not ... they didn't take any interest really.

She left school at 15 and worked in routine clerical work. She became pregnant at 18, prior to her marriage and told me she still remembers the shame of it:

First of all when I was pregnant, I was desperate not to have a baby. I just didn't want to get married. But I couldn't speak to my parents, my father definitely not and my mother, who would have been very embarrassed and I'd brought shame on the family so I just had to get married. And you have to cover yourself up, you know, to hope that when you've had the baby nobody notices you've been pregnant.

I felt so ashamed of myself that I went through with it. And I didn't want to. I didn't want the baby and I certainly didn't want to get married ... my parents were fairly strict and you just, you didn't argue because they didn't understand. So there was no point in trying to talk to them, they didn't understand at all.

I asked her why she felt so guilty about being pregnant and again, her response was a reflection of the social pressure she had already described:

Because first of all to have sex before marriage, I was made to feel absolutely dirty and because, because of all the moral issues and my upbringing. My parents were so much against it. Not being married at eighteen, they quite accepted that because really, looking back in 1966, a lot of my friends were married at eighteen, nineteen.

So it wasn't that, it was just actually having sex before you were married or being found out and having a baby. And it was shameful for my parents to meet the neighbours. You know, what would the neighbours think and the family, and I was just made to feel so ashamed of myself. When I went to the clinic, before we got married and they knew I wasn't married, they still called your name as 'Mrs'. so again you got the shame thing, the guilt thing again, that you should have been married.

Bryony had difficulty in accepting her new identity which was located in the home and her caring responsibilities:

> I got married in April and my son was born at the end of August. I didn't have any help in looking after him because I'd had him and, you know, you've made your bed and you lie on it now. So I didn't have any help so there's no way I could have gone back to work, but it nearly drove me mad with my first child. I just wanted to go back to work. I don't know whether I really wanted him. But looking back on it, I did want him, I just needed to get back out for a few days a week or something. And so my husband then suggested 'why don't you go to keep fit classes - something like that?' Being physical again, that was the turning point I think really, because I then did go to the local keep fit class and that led on to eventually my movement training.

I asked Bryony why she had chosen to return to education and do the course she was doing now. She told me that she had been helping her husband establish a business. He had had a severe car accident about fifteen years ago and almost died; the driver of the other car did die. He was hospitalised for four months and was then made redundant. They set up and ran a party-plan furnishing business for several years and eventually they set up a similar business in a shop, which he now runs, although she does the accounts and the personnel work. She told me they did not work well together, but she enjoyed the personnel work, which means, as she told me: 'I can keep clear, well away from him'. It also gave her the opportunity to do a full-time course. She told me that she had done several courses before she enrolled for her current science access course, but because these were mostly connected with her fitness teaching, she did not really regard them as academic:

> I'd never taken GCSEs and I was married at eighteen. I had three children, the first when I was nineteen, the second at twenty one and the third when I was twenty seven so I feel like I've not really had much of an education. I've been waiting really to come back, even though I've done things in between - but the proper academic side I've been waiting.

Although Bryony's husband was encouraging and supportive of the training involved in her fitness work, he is not happy about her return to academic education, even though it is something which she has wanted to do for a long time. She feels that this is because they have different values and because of his lack of understanding of her need for mental stimulation and challenge:

> He can't understand why I want to do it. He can't understand why I don't want to get a job and earn money, because money is more important to him than it is to me. It would help if I worked and brought some money in which I did when my daughter was at university, to help with the fees and that. But I found that working as a telephonist and being a telephonist/receptionist was not challenging enough and I was bored out of my mind.

> So when my husband suggested that I do something again, like that, I just couldn't face it.   I can't face twenty years of working a switchboard and filing because I'm not qualified to do anything, but I feel I'm capable of doing more. I think he may feel that now the children are older he can't understand why I just don't want to go and get any job - because he can't see the point in what I'm doing. He thinks it's a waste of time, and a year here and three years at higher education is just a waste of time when I could be earning money. We have different views on it.

Even though Bryony's aim is a 'better' job, she has no clear idea of what that might be. It seems she simply wants to fulfil her potential:

> I want to get myself an education, even though it's late, and I want to, not particularly go on to do a degree, I'm not bothered about that, I want to get some qualifications that would lead to an interesting job. Something challenging. Something interesting that I haven't sussed out in a day.

She has not found the course easy, but she has not considered giving it up. Her confidence was low when the course started, but has improved considerably:

> The first day I felt shocking, terrible. Because, going in the first morning and first of all going in a hall with all the sixteen year olds as well, they looked as I walked in, because obviously they thought at my age I was the tutor, you see. So I felt like a fish out of water really. Dreadful, absolutely. It took quite a while, it took months actually, but Christmas was the turning point when I started to feel better.

Bryony is continuing with her course despite experiencing considerable domestic pressure. It seems that she has been striving for most of her adult life for some independence, autonomy and power to define her own identity outside the home, and an academic education is the vehicle she is using. Although she has been successful in her fitness courses and teaching, this is clearly not enough for her. She does not regard this as a 'real' education which will expand her mind and develop her thinking, rather she sees it as training for a specific reason and she is determined to take the opportunities she feels she threw away in her childhood. This, I felt, was just as important to her as her aim for a more fulfilling job. When the tape was switched off, she told me that she felt too old, at 46, to do the course, but she is fighting her husband's control and is determined to complete her studies. She is clearly wanting to establish an identity over which she has more influence than she has had hitherto.

Frances

Frances' social and economic circumstances differ from those of Bryony. She lives in an area of high unemployment, which is designated deprived by the European Social Fund and in receipt of funding for community provision. The courses are free at the community training and education centre and Frances has been a part-time student for the past two years. She is currently studying a validated equivalent of A-level English, and goes to a woodwork class, one morning a week. Her compulsory education was in a comprehensive school, and her unplanned pregnancy started whilst she was still there, not through ignorance, but through embarrassment about buying contraceptives. She delayed telling her mother because of family circumstances:

> Frances: When I got pregnant in the first place, I didn't dare tell my mum because my Nan had just had a stroke - my mum's not a strong person and I thought well that's all she needs, she'll just have a breakdown or something. So I didn't tell them. So I was about seven months, when it was too late to do anything. I just used to wear my coat all the time.
>
> I had her in the April, and it was a February and we were on a mountain walk ... and it was like five foot deep in snow and I thought, 'what am I doing here?' And they'd got, like, big plastic bags, you know, when it was break, we sat in those 'cos it was that cold. And I thought, 'honestly, what am I doing here?' I just felt like stopping in mine and dying. I must've been mad. And it would have been a bit after that, that I told my twin sister, Liza - we were in a French lesson and I said to Liza, 'I've got something to tell you'. She says, 'What?' I says, 'I'm pregnant'. She says, 'Christ, Frances!' in front of all the class. She just didn't believe me. She was like

mesmerised and it was actually one of the teachers what took me home, and told my mum.

Social attitudes, particularly among the older generation, were reflected in her father's attitude towards the pregnancy, and she had to leave home when the baby was born:

> My dad was alive then - how many years ago then, fourteen, fifteen - it isn't such a crime now as it used to be in the old days. Dad didn't say anything – 'cos he was a lot older than my mum - I think he was about twenty five years older than her - and he just looked and went into the other room. You know, like they do, stormed off. And that was that. Then he said, 'Oh well you've got to leave home. You've got to get married'. And I didn't want to but I went to live with Shelly's dad - I stopped at home till the day I went into labour and after that I had to live with him.

This relationship was fairly short-lived, and she lived on her own for some time, on the estate where she still lives:

> I was with him till Shelly was about eighteen months, and then I'd just had enough, I left him. He used to be a heavy drinker, he was a lot older than me, t'final straw was he was womanising with this other woman and I walked round the corner and there they were, holding hands. I thought I'm not standing for this any more and I left - even then I didn't go back home. We'd just moved on to the Greenfield then, and he'd left me with this house that was just going to be modernised. I had to do all the decorating, see to all the builders, look after Shelly and it was awful - but it was still better than living with him.

Frances has lived with her current partner for six years, but it would appear to be an uneasy alliance. She receives separate income as a single parent, and appears to take full responsibility for domestic chores and childcare. Her partner is not particularly happy with her return to education and this manifests itself in his refusal to help with the children, even though he is at home most of the day. She feels this is a deliberate attempt to control her:

> I wouldn't claim with Steve because he thinks his money's for going to the pub and drinking. If we had to rely on his money, I don't know how much he'd give me but he's just not grown up enough or mature enough to handle things like that.

At one bit, before we had Mark we was going to get married and I just couldn't. He never put me first. If he was more reliable ... I just couldn't go through with it. I'm classed as a single parent but 'cos he's there, it's handy when I can't get to pick Mark up from school or anything, you know, if he's there - 'well you go and pick him up'. But at one time, when he was having to take him we had a terrible row. 'I'm not taking him to school and I'm not picking him up'. I was in a right flap thinking who I could get to do it for me. It was going to be another day that I wasn't going to be in you see. So he said he wouldn't do it. And sometimes, because Sandy's not his daughter, it's all 'it's your daughter, you do it'.

However, she has refused to let this prevent her attendance at the centre:

This is my third year now so he's used to it, but at first, well he, and his family were the same. 'I don't know, what you going for? What do you want, when you pass exams what you going to do?' He didn't like it, but he saw that I wasn't going to stop it just because he didn't like it and I suppose he's come round to the idea now.

For Frances, education provides, many things. Firstly, she sees her return to education as something very much for herself. She very much enjoys courses which give her a life and identity out of home:

I do English. We're doing advanced literature first - Open College. Then on Wednesdays I've got a part time job, which is opening the workshop up at the community centre for the woodwork and I do woodwork on Wednesdays. I was absolutely bored and fed up. And I thought 'well it's better than watching tele' so I might go and have a go at that because it's something to do. So I thought well, I like reading, I spend most of my time reading, so I'm doing English.

Secondly, she is proud of her achievement:

He went to the social the other week and he was filling a form out for something and when it got to the exam bit I said, 'Well two years ago I wouldn't have been able to put anything down where it says qualifications. But now I can put GCSE English Language and Literature'. He says, 'alright, alright'. I says, 'now you can see why I'm going?'

I just got my certificates last week, it came through and I put them on the wall, and it's something to be proud of - something for yourself and not what they've, not for them. My daughter says 'oh look she's bragging again'. I said, 'well you'd brag if you'd done it'.

Thirdly, Frances' achievement has boosted her confidence. I asked her if she had plans to move on from the neighbourhood centre:

> At first it put me off 'cos I thought, well I were right goon when I were young. You know, I know that's not the case now, I mean, you get to know people. I actually went down to college to a women's studies do, they had an evening, and that was quite good - loads of people older than me and I thought, 'well I won't be the only one'. So I might, it just depends. I really don't know what I want to do with my life. I could go to university if I managed to get a place, the tutor says ...

Fourthly, she also recognises that education may be the only way she can get out of her current situation:

> I think, if you've got a better education - I mean, it might sound snobbish or something - but the better your chances are of having a house of your own one day instead of living on a council estate. I hated it on here when I first moved ...

Finally though, the main point she makes is that what she is doing is for herself:

> It's interest. I'm interested in the work that we do in English and I like writing, and I'd like to probably, one day, if I could, write a book. I mean, I've got plenty of things to put in but it's just putting them down. I think it was just interest. It's nice to have something to do other than - something you want to do other than things that have to be done. I like doing it. You've got a life out of home haven't you?

Frances is gaining many benefits from her education, all of which are linked with her striving for some independence and an identity which she is defining, rather than it being defined by others. It is interesting that she lives in a very restrictive environment, but has carved out an independent identity within that framework. Although her unplanned pregnancy had a major impact on her life, this in itself is not now the central issue, rather it is her relationship with her partner which is the ongoing problem.

Jenny

Jenny is 37, married with three children. She lives in the same area and attends the same neighbourhood centre as Frances. She has been studying here for about three years, on a variety of courses such as English, typing, office practice - whatever the centre offers, she is prepared to enrol for. The courses are free, supported by the European Social Fund because this is a designated deprived area. She is very aware of the social and cultural constraints on her life and is frustrated not only by private control, exerted within her family, but also public control - through socialisation, cultural norms within her neighbourhood and her perception of attitudes in the wider society, particularly in respect of the benefits system. She took GCEs when she was in mainstream education, but became pregnant shortly after she had started a course in nursery nursing:

> Jenny: I was pregnant. I'd been going out with Trev from being thirteen, absolutely green because we'd got no sex education whatsoever; we was an exam group so you wasn't given the sex education. I was sixteen when I got married, and seventeen when I had my oldest baby. When we were married, the powers that be told my husband that he was my legal guardian so that were it ... and I kind of let him. I got some real flak off my mum when I were pregnant and getting married - one of my aunts were actually cheeky enough to say, 'What you marrying that scrubber for? It's beneath you'. There were all that pressure.
>
> I go down to my mum's now and she says, 'she's throwing her life away', and I'm thinking 'they're not telling me nothing I can't see', but I'm in a catch 22 situation. I married Trev because I loved him not 'cos I were pregnant but, now sometimes, 'you've thrown a career away', er, 'why han't you done this?' 'It's a shame, you're wasting your life' and everything. And there's Trev sat back saying, 'Er, yeah, and I'm here'.

Jenny's husband has been ill, suffering from depression, for the last thirteen years of their twenty year marriage and she told me he is very resentful of her return to education. What she is talking about here is the conflicting attitudes between her extended family members who feel she continues to 'waste her life', and her husband who reminds her that his needs have to be considered. He is constantly reminding her by both words and actions that he has considerable control over her life:

> I can't actually see Trev getting well and going out to work again, but we're in a dog-in-t'manger situation - he doesn't want me to. He's a qualified motor mechanic but he had a nervous breakdown which made him agoraphobic and he's been home now for thirteen years - and I've looked after him. He couldn't even go in the garden unless I went in the garden with him. In between that thirteen year I've had two more babies. One's got minor motor damage and some growth motor damage - the youngest; the other one's acute asthmatic, so I

have to be there to see to them. He could see to them in the house,
but he won't.

Jenny attempts to play down her progress and enjoyment of the
course, but her husband's resentment of her education appears to have
grown recently and he threatened divorce. This resulted in her breaking
down in the doctor's surgery:

> It's stressful now and I've got to see a community psychiatric nurse
> because of the stress. I actually collapsed in the doctor's because he
> knows that I am developing more - and trying to keep that bit
> subdued is hard. He'll not come when I get anything, but he'll not
> acknowledge that I've got a certificate. Not long ago all the students
> who took the RSA exam were put in the Austen Journal. I'm four foot
> ten so I get stuck on the front row don't I? And people are saying, 'I
> saw you in the paper', and I'm thinking 'oh my God', and his face - I
> could literally see it slipping more and more. But the argument is that
> he knew I wasn't stupid when he married me. I tell him 'I'm not the
> little woman that sits there sewing'.

> Things've really come to a head, you know, these last few months, so
> much so that he actually threatened me with divorce. That's how
> serious it's just got you see, so I've got to re-educate Trev else I ...

I asked how she managed to return to education if he was so much
against it:

> I came out while he was on tablets. I'm not saying it was easy, I was
> actually a battered wife at one time. I'm four foot ten and Trev's six
> foot four, so there's a big difference in size ... he still, now he's gone
> from physical to mental. He doesn't realise he's doing it but it's the
> same type of thing. Well I presume he doesn't because he knows that
> I've got to see somebody and he knows that there's something wrong,
> that I'm getting to nearly screaming stage at times.

As well as the private control, Jenny is also very aware of the public
influence on a woman's identity once she is married. She is clearly
resentful of her loss of individuality:

> You lose your identity. You stop being a person when you get
> married and especially when she's had that first baby, she becomes a
> non-person. You don't become anybody. I suppose at the age I was
> then, and it was early seventies, I didn't fit in. Now there's quite a
> few unmarried mothers. When I took Rick to nursery the mothers
> were older, so they looked at me as if I were a bit of dirt that had
> crawled from under a stone - even my sister-in-law, who'd got one at

nursery at t'same time. The only people I found that ever did take any notice were some of the staff, 'cos they knew I'd done the nursery nursing. So, of course, I were handy for voluntary helper - do the painting and that. But then I wasn't called Jenny, I was called Rick's mum, or Trev's wife. And you want to stand on a pedestal and shout, 'look at me - there's me here. I am somebody if you'd take notice'.

Jenny is very aware of the neighbourhood norms which not only influences her husband's attitude but also serves to define her identity and lay some limitations on what she can do:

We don't go out much 'cos of Trev's illness but I've noticed if we do go out the women sit down and have a drink when the male goes and fetches it. Alright he might fetch her one glass of lager say, but the second drink he doesn't say 'do you want anything different?' My favourite trick is when we have been out I change a drink every drink. Trev knows this and I blooming drive him nuts, absolutely drives him crazy but it's just this perverse little thing - notice me! I might only be a woman, but I've got a mind.

Trev's always kept me on a tight rein, never let me go out. I've never been to night clubs and things like this, but letting the man go for a drink, well he's a man, been working all day - it's acceptable. If you go in a pub, all eyes are on you. You're either two things - you're either on the game as they put it, or some bloody bloke's not got you in control ... your husband's under t'thumb or he's a wimp or whatever they want to call them, and that's just because you go for a drink.

This area that we're in now, this estate, it's still accepted that the man's the one that's the breadwinner. If the woman goes out then he's looked down on, so there's all that peer pressure to the males, 'what you doing letting her go out?' type of thing. It's high unemployment round here, they just don't accept that there's a partnership. They were always brought up that the males went to work. My husband's one of six. I'm not saying they're uneducated but my mum-in-law's gone out cleaning, that's what was accepted. She were always in for the kids. In this area you'll find a lot of 'em's like that. They've always been there for the kids. They're not a good mother if they're not, you know? It don't matter whether they've laid on the floor, like I lay on the floor and do homework with my kids, but that don't make me a good mother. At the end of the day, if my kids have a hot meal, if they're clean when they go to school, if I'm there to pick them up, that makes you a good mother, that makes you accepted by society otherwise you're not accepted, you're like an outcast.

Everybody, I don't care who they are, everybody has to conform to society in some ways, or life's made hard for you, really hard. But it's not just made hard for you. I consider that I'm a good mother but if I wasn't there for my kids the kids would be made to feel that I'm a bad mother as well. So it snowballs the effect.

Even Jenny's return to education is tempered by what she sees as acceptable within the community in which she lives. She contrasts this with her own family's background and attitudes and acknowledges that it causes her continual conflict:

So rather than stay at home I went into education (but) I'm on call now for t'phone. In the last six months I bet I've been called out about twelve times - out of lessons, out of t'centre. It's a kind of draw - you've still got that string attached that you feel as though you're neglecting your family. It's what society puts on you, it's like a mental hold. The woman looks after the family and if you are not there for them you're neglecting them ... I just can't accept that is all you're meant to do in life, because I know it's not.

In my family the women have always worked. The women have always gone into education. I'm not saying we're brilliantly educated but we're middle of the road education, so to me it's fairly natural.

My great-grandma were a school teacher - which is not acceptable in a lot of the society that Trev comes from. On both sides, on my father's side and my mother's, it's different, a different life. It's really hard you know, I suppose I'm like stuck in no-man's land trying to merge - if it were Trev that were doing these courses and wanting to go on I would back him - and people would expect me to back him, yet because I'm female and it's me that's got - I suppose it's some type of drive - I'm seen as a freak - you shouldn't do it.

As well as the private control of her husband and the public control of the neighbourhood in which she lives, Jenny feels that her opportunities are also restricted because of the structure of the benefits system. I have discussed this in chapter five, but the point which she makes is that any benefits which she receives personally could make the family worse off financially. I asked Jenny why, given that there were so many pressures on her, she had come back into education. She has aspirations but they are tinged with realism:

I've been working at the school now for seven or eight year on a voluntary basis, teaching special needs. I would love to either go into hospitals and work within an 'ospital or work within a school. But who's going to let me get that education at the end of the day? People say 'it's up to you' but no, it's not up to you. You find the doors shut, you know? My age now is going against me, I suppose, I'm thirty seven. If I was to go teaching - it's a three year course, I'm forty. What school's going to accept a forty year old against somebody at twenty six?

If the government bring where mothers can go in and do their qualifications while they work, and make it worthwhile that people can work, then that would be great for me. But I am restricted to here. I'd love to do some type of research which I'd need to go to university or some type of higher education establishment. (but) I can't see a college being pleased if you get a phone call that says will you come out of college, t'little one's having an asthma attack!

And I can't see him (her husband) letting me go on a campus life. I have a bit of social life at the centre when they have the parties, the Christmas parties and that, but you're still limited. You hear the government say, 'look at this, you'll have a carefree life at university and everything'. You only need somebody like Trev watching that and 'there's no way my wife's doing that, type of thing'. So you're limited. The English teacher keeps pushing me - why don't I do more? but you're stopped at every turn.

I've still got family pressures, I've still got Trev's illness. I've still got government pressures because they're saying everybody's got an equal opportunity - but no you haven't. You can't make your family worse off than what they are, and the benefits that you get goes on what your husband earns, or what he's entitled to.

Janet: So this is more than about job prospects then?

Jenny: It is. It's not just job prospects. With what I've got, without bragging, I could get a decent job. I know I could go further but every bend that you turn, every corner you turn, there's either society - because of ways that they've been brought up - or there's a government department that stops you.

I'm a female. Nobody's going to hold their hand out to me and say, 'You've got to work, you need to work to support your family, aren't you doing a good job?'.

There is an also an element of having to prove her ability to her extended family:

> I like to prove people wrong I suppose. What started me on was my mum had a party. Now my mum can be very cruel and my twin sister's always been the main one, and we went to this, something like a women's gathering and somebody happened to turn round to me and say, 'oh how's Trev and Rick?' And I says, 'Oh they're great' and my mum turned round and said, 'don't take no notice of our Jenny, she's no topic of conversation only Trev and the kids'. And I thought 'I'll show you'. I admit sometimes now when I get a certificate, I kind of put it there and I'll say, 'oh I've just passed this, I've just done ... '.

She has tremendous pride in her achievement and a determination not to give it up:

> Alright it has made me ill but if I give way then what have I achieved with all these years? I've not achieved nothing. I might as well have just said, 'I've gone back to that person who sits in a corner and does nothing', which I'm not willing to do. Alright I might not get chance to do much with it but at least I know I've achieved something - I've got enough certificates now to nearly plaster a wall.

She is also developing a new identity through the knowledge she has acquired from her education. This gives her a certain amount of higher status in the neighbourhood and within her family:

> I did one course, social studies ... so I know how to look the law up and I find that they're coming to me now for advice and I keep wanting to say, 'but I've no topic of conversation', but you know, you bite your tongue just to let things go. But I think that were where it started and people just ignoring me - 'don't take no notice of her - what's she doing?'.

Jenny suggests it is her own obstinacy and determination not to give in to the social pressure which makes her continue to do what she is doing:

> I'm bloody minded I suppose. If I want something ... you've got to work at it. I were once described as having a male ego. Now I don't know whether that were insult or what, but if I wasn't like that I think I would have given in. I think they meant I was just strong minded, to some extent. I'm not that strong minded, it does hurt when they're being nasty, but I'm good at putting a front on. Luckily I've never broke down here (at the centre).

There is also a fight to exert more control over her own life and for some independence, both from her husband and his family:

> When Trev said our marriage was over, been over for three or four months, I took him at word and it were just the last straw. Now what he's saying is, 'but it is over if you continue your education'. So I'm kind of digging my heels in and thinking, 'you need me more than I need you'. He'd pulled the reins in. I'm just stretching the reins now do you know? I do tug at the bit quite often. I'm seen as, not a freak or anything but something with my husband's family. 'What's she doing now? How can she do that?' So it's fighting all way.

Education appears to be Jenny's lifeline. These remarks were scattered throughout the interview:

> I'm doing these courses now, they're not all what I want to do. I'm not a typist but there's a course that's on offer here – while ever there's courses running here, I shall take them.

> You need something like this. If it's only to keep your brain going, you know?

> I have fought for what I've got. People don't realise how hard you have to fight.

> You've got to be a strong individual to get on.

> I'm rebelling - if I hadn't, I would have folded, I would have folded.

> It's the way that I escape the unfairness I suppose.

Clearly for Jenny, education is linked with her apparently desperate need for some independence and to have some control over how her own identity is defined. Her story reflects and reinforces those of many of the women, though Jenny's verbalisation of her feelings is rather more explicit than some of the others have been. Her last point about fairness, is also a central issue in Sheila's story, which appears in the next chapter.

Summary

Unplanned pregnancy has had a major effect on the lives of these four students and was associated with repressive relationships. These controlling relationships are linked with the students' return to education in terms of a need for independence and control over their identity. As with the last group of students, this independence is linked with a resistance to the power and control of significant others. They have taken very different courses but have common links between their lives and their return to education.

Claire's car maintenance course is important to her because it means that she is no longer defined as dependent in this particularly male dominated area. For Bryony and Frances, the need for independence is linked with a resistance to the power and control of their partners to define their identity as primarily located within a domestic setting. Jenny is not only resisting her partner's control, she is also determined not to allow the neighbourhood culture to totally determine her identity. In addition, the new respect she is gaining from her family is also giving her a more positive self-image.

For all the women, working within very different frameworks, the major link with education was the desire to exert more control over their lives than they have previously had. Education has served this purpose for all of them, in different ways, regardless of the course on which they are enrolled. With this increasing control, as with the students in the previous group, has come an increase in confidence and a more positive self-image.

7 Mega trauma and the links with education

Independence, control over their lives, and the connections between these and identity are the three major links which the group of students in this chapter also make with education. For these students, traumatic experiences started early and have often continued, perhaps in different forms throughout their lives. As with the other students, the stories are very individual, but they all talk of confidence, a more positive self-image, self-fulfilment and independence. The stories are of psychological trauma, physical abuse, and sometimes both. What separates these students from the others are the major and seemingly ongoing effects of their painful experiences. Gerry, who told me of the ongoing effects of the abuse she experienced, begins the chapter.

Gerry

Gerry is 26, single, with no children and lives at home with her parents. She left school at 16 and entered further education, training as a chef. She started work at 19, mostly short-term, part-time work 'cheffing/waitressing'. She told me that she lost her penultimate job as a casino waitress largely because 'I was too big, I didn't fit the image they wanted to promote in their casino' (she weighed 24 stones at the time). Her last job as a holiday temp. at a local university spurred her into enrolling for an access course which she completed last year. She is currently enrolled on the foundation year of a 4-year combined studies degree course at a local college - the following three years being undertaken at a local university.

Gerry links the start of her problems with the family home move from Scotland to Derbyshire. She was also aware of the long-term effects of some of her difficulties:

> ...we moved to Derbyshire from Scotland and I had a heavy Scottish accent and I was complete outcast because of that plus the fact everybody had been to primary school together and here was this

person from outside coming in trying to make friends with people ...
It wasn't up until the last year of school I actually made proper
friends and even then it was only a couple of them.

I personally think a lot of people tend to carry a lot of baggage with
them through life you know from previous things that have happened
you build up this sort of stigma which is attached. You're like a
social outcast and it tends to affect the way you think about yourself
mentally. Obviously trying to make friends with lots of sweets I put
on an awful lot of weight which in turn affects again the way people
look at me. My sister was particularly nasty towards me at that time
obviously venting her frustrations on me to the point where we
literally very rarely spoke to each other. It was hate ... and that added
to the problems as well I know.

She went on to tell me about the sexual abuse she experienced in her
childhood and its effect on her:

From the period age 11 through to 12, I was sexually abused for a
year. My brother was responsible for that and that is something that
at the time obviously I hadn't a clue what was going on. I didn't
recognise or understand the consequences of what was going on and
in fact I didn't actually speak to anybody about what happened until I
was about 21 or 22. I never mentioned it to anybody and that really
just messed me up completely - totally affected my attitude. I didn't
realise it then but looking at it now I realise it has affected to a huge
extent the way I look on things and the way I look on what has
happened in my life and how I deal with those things ... I have so
many reservations about 'will I get hurt', 'what will happen', 'what
do these people want from me', 'what do I want from myself', that I
find it increasingly difficult at times ... I find it very difficult to go
into a totally different social setting and create new friends and I just
find whatever I try and decide, whatever decision it is in my life
whether it be big or small is affected by what's happened in the past.

I'm trying to sort of come away from that and leave the past behind
which is very difficult to do because the memory's constantly there.
In particular I have a real problem with situations where I'm in a
male orientated environment. I have a high level of aggression which
I constantly have to keep in check and I'm constantly running things
through my mind all the time which makes it very difficult when I'm
sat in a lesson and I'm trying to listen to somebody telling me all this
information and I have all this other stuff going round in my mind.

She went on to link her school experiences and her abuse and then talks about the long-term difficulties they created for her:

The two main reasons for why I put weight on in the first place was because one was carrying a lot of sweets round to make friends and the other was to try and hide myself hide away from men in particular because I felt that if I was big, men wouldn't want to come near me. When you're young, fair enough but when you get older you suddenly start to realise its not as clear cut as that and then you get the situation where you want a relationship but you daren't have a relationship because you don't know how you would react and you get this vicious circle building up and you go round and round and round until you just don't know where you are. You don't know where the beginning is, you don't know where the end is, you just go round and round in a circle and the more you worry the more you get depressed the more you come down on yourself the worse it gets.

I got to a stage when I was sort of 16, 17 - I ran away from home while I was at school a couple of times ... and it was all these questions 'why did you do it, tell us?' I was so mixed up I didn't know what to tell them. I just said 'I don't know'. I couldn't tell them what had been happening. It would have absolutely torn their whole world apart. It would have made things even worse and it would made me feel worse and I couldn't have handled it.

I tried to commit suicide twice. The first time I actually sat on a window ledge three storeys up thinking 'I'll jump out' and I hadn't the courage to do it. The second time I actually had a knife at my wrists and I was ready for cutting my wrists and my brother came into the room. We had a struggle and I ended up cutting my thumb instead. A few years later I took a load of tablets but unfortunately I'd taken a load of vitamin tablets thinking that this was it - I was going to finish with life and all they did were make me feel extremely sick for about two days.

In her early twenties, Gerry began to have counselling for depression, which the counsellor assumed was because of her weight. It took Gerry a year to tell the counsellor about her experiences and she found that in itself fairly traumatic:

I didn't know where I was as a person or what I wanted to do with life. I was just aimlessly going along from one thing to another and when I got kicked in the teeth, desperately tried to pick myself up and carry on with the next thing, without really thinking about what it was and where it was I wanted to go. It just seemed like a natural way -

you get knocked down and get on with the next thing. It's quite frightening when you start talking. The first time I talked to that counsellor and I started talking about how I actually felt, that was quite frightening and quite difficult to come to terms with all the feelings that have built up over the years.

Gerry's problems continued when she returned to education and although she recognises the origins of them, they are still painful:

I think I went through a lot of problems when I was on the access course because previously I'd been involved with a man for the first relationship that I had had - purely platonic but he let me down quite badly. I found he was already living with somebody else, so the one fella I started to trust betrayed that trust. Then I got involved with another gentleman, well I wouldn't call him a gentleman because he wasn't a gentleman, on the access course and that was actually a physical relationship from the word go and I think it was almost a case of I was so desperate to have a relationship, that kind of relationship with somebody, I just threw myself into it and I had all sorts of problems when that relationship broke up because I went through all the same feelings that I had all those years ago that I was worthless, that I was a failure, that I couldn't cope with anything and so I found the last few months in particular of the access course very difficult.

Gerry still does not feel able to be open about the abuse she experienced and she has conflicting emotions about her brother, which she finds difficult to handle:

My brother and I have a curious relationship we have never ever spoken of what happened - as far as he's concerned, consciously and openly it didn't happen. I have no doubt that in the deep dark recesses of his mind it is there and every so often he will be reminded of it, but when I was going out with Phil on the access course, he said to me 'well you're innocent, you've never done anything before' ... I've come so close to saying 'but don't you remember this?' and stopped myself. I think more than anything now because he is actually married and he's got a settled life and I think if I brought it up now it wouldn't just affect him it would affect his wife and I couldn't live with that. I love my brother dearly and if anything happened to him I would be there like a shot but at the same time I hate his guts and I have real problems at times when I see him and his wife together. I hate the happiness that he's got and the success that he's got and I get very angry at that, very angry. Again these are all

things that a few years ago I wouldn't have admitted to, I wouldn't
have even recognised that was the reason why I felt the way I did or
how I felt really, but we get along like an ordinary brother and sister.
It's only when we argue that the difference comes to light because the
aggression I have towards him comes out and there have been a
number of times when he said 'I can't understand why you are so
aggressive towards me', and I think 'oh God, don't you realise?' He
doesn't realise the effect it's had.

Gerry told me that her unwillingness to reveal her brother's part in
the abuse is partly to protect herself. Again, her ambivalent feelings show
through:

I couldn't tell my parents who it was because it would tear their
world apart and I couldn't do that because it would hurt me because
the people who are most central to my life are my parents. At the end
of the day my family are the most important thing in my life. They
are the only thing that have given me any continuity and I cling to
that to the extent that I won't hear a word said against them. I get
really angry if people comment even on my brother. To tell them that
it was actually my brother would actually rip the family apart and I
think know after all these years although it might give me some
personal satisfaction to some extent and it might help me in some
way to lift that burden it would also create other burdens that I
couldn't live with.

Since she has been receiving counselling, Gerry has become part of a
help-line network for victims of abuse and she went on to tell me of a client
who had named her family abuser and was ostracised by her family. This
had reinforced Gerry's decision to keep quiet about her brother.

I asked her why she decided to do the course now and she told me
that her decision to study sciences on the access course had been a mistake,
and although she had passed, she had realised over the year that she wanted
to work with people in a caring situation, but there is also a major element
of proving her ability:

Well I felt that if I didn't do it now I would never do it and I sort of
came to a point where I thought 'I can either carry on the way that I
am going and make a total mess of my life or try and get something
positive from the negative' - try to get to a position where I can
actually carry on with my life ... I think more than anything because I
fear this sort of inferiority. My sister and my brother have both got
degrees but I hadn't got that kind of qualification and I think
probably in the back of my mind I was feeling that I had to prove

myself, not just to them but to myself ... that spurred me on - perhaps this was a way I could prove to myself, more to myself than anybody else that I wasn't a failure. Even if I didn't actually succeed it was something that I actually got the courage to go and try and to have a go at ...

Interwoven with the need to prove her ability is her desire to exercise power and control over her life:

To some extent I've made progress. I'd actually decided for myself instead of other people deciding for me, to go on the access course. It was a decision I'd made rather than other people which was something that hadn't really happened before. So I'm going to see it through so I can say to myself I'd done it against all the odds against anything that's happened I've come through the other side and I've actually achieved something. My mum will tell you that I felt really proud the first year when I got my credits and I took my mum and my brother and my sister-in-law along to the presentation evening because I wanted them to be there I wanted some of my family to see the fact that I had actually achieved something. I mean in the scheme of things it wasn't very much but to me it was a lot.

Gerry's ongoing painful experiences are still having an effect on her. Returning to education is enabling her to take some control over her life and is helping her to build a new image, a large part of which is tied up with proving her ability, both to herself and to others. She told me 'I felt very daunted when I first came back into education', and although she did not talk specifically about her growing confidence during the taped interview, it is implicit in what she said throughout. I gave Gerry a lift to the bus stop after the interview and she told me that she was determined to do something with her life, to get her degree and to work with people. She also told me she was dieting and had lost some weight. This, together with her reference to courage, is an indication of how much she has moved forward since she has been at college.

Petra

Petra's painful experiences are also rooted in her childhood. She is 40, married with no children, and currently in the third year of a four year degree course which carries a social work qualification at a local university. She had a secondary school education and although she could have transferred at 13, she remained where she was and left school at 14 with no qualifications:

I failed my 11+. At 13 I got a chance to transfer to the grammar school but I don't think it would have worked out because by this time my mother was an alcoholic ... so I most certainly wouldn't have got the support I needed. I can remember having this piece of paper for them to sign so I could go and I had it in my pocket for ages and I showed it to them then put it back into my pocket - it's so strange now - I can remember feeling a bit hurt with the fact that nobody took it seriously. .

As she implies here, it was the effects of her mother's alcoholism rather than the alcoholism itself which were the problem. Her mother started drinking when Petra was around 11 and was drinking heavily two years later. Petra had to take responsibility for her sister, who was 8 years her junior, and report her behaviour to her father who worked shifts and could not be there all the time. She feels that this supervisory and controlling role still affects her relationship with her sister:

It was difficult for me because when my sister was about 5 she (her mother) was quite heavily into her drinking so I had to take on responsibility for my sister. It was a lot of responsibility because I was very young, my father worked shifts. It really affected our relationship a bit because I don't think I was particularly good at it. I was only a child myself but I used to have to report things she'd done because she was a very strong willed child and she was quite naughty and I used to have to tell me dad about things she'd done. She remembers that now and if she tells me something in confidence she'll say 'I know you'll tell my dad', and I say 'of course I won't tell my dad, I used to have to do it when you were getting in the ice cream van and going for a ride round the block with the ice cream man - of course I did - you should be able to work that out for yourself now' but she still doesn't quite trust me ...

The situation worsened considerably and Petra went to live with her grandparents, visiting her mother occasionally:

It actually got worse because for two years it was really like hell on earth. Julie used to want to come with me everywhere and I didn't want it, but I knew my mother wouldn't harm her other than out of neglect. I mean I can look back now and see of course it was a harmful situation but I said 'no, you'll be alright with her and I won't be too long' or 'I shan't be late' and I used to leave her and I would get home and the neighbours had fetched her so she was obviously a very frightened little girl. Eventually the doctor said to my father that he would have to sort something out otherwise it would be a case of us having to move out and I actually had to live with my grandparents. They didn't want my sister - she was seen as a bit of a handful ... but after a few weeks of us all being split up Julie eventually came to us and about a year later my dad came as well ... I used to go round Sunday mornings to see her because she wasn't drunk then - that was the best time ...

By this time Petra had left school and was working as a tracer in a local engineering company. She was still taking a large part of the responsibility for her sister and was finding the whole situation more and more difficult:

So we were all living there and it was obviously far too much for her (her grandmother) ... I was about 19 ... I used to do as much as I could, more than my sister and dad. My dad had carried my mum all these years doing housework etc. but once he got back home he didn't do anything - sat in the arm chair and Julie was still the baby. I used to get Julie up for school before I went to work and I used to help out with washing and stuff. I used to go back into Austen on a Saturday with my Grandma to help her with the shopping ... the whole situation deteriorated. I had relatives in Hull and a boyfriend and I used to go over to cousins and I had a very good social life. He understood the situation totally as he had lost his mother and he suggested I move there which I did. Got a job and it was 'what is she doing? why is she doing this?' and no one understood it. I don't think people understand it to this day ... An aunt told me only a couple of years ago she thought my lot (then) was alright, which shocked me ...

Petra still has guilt feelings about leaving her sister and takes much of the responsibility for what she sees as her sister's emotional problems:

Julie stopped where she was ... and it changed the relationship until she got married herself. She was just devastated because I had gone ... She finds it difficult to show her emotion, she couldn't put her arm round me to say well done - she always sends me a good luck card before my exams but that's the most she can do ...

After her marriage when she was 20, Petra moved around the country quite a lot for her husband's work, but her painful experiences did not end:

It was a really traumatic time generally. I'd really been brought up by my gran because of my mum but the day we moved down to Twyford she had a heart attack and died three days later and I was really upset - I'd left all my friends behind ...

Tim was head hunted and he decided to move to this job in London and it was an absolute nightmare, he only stayed about three months and we went to Peterborough and unfortunately that job didn't work out at all and they just got rid of a load of people and he was one ...

He'd got extremely bad angina and the stupid doctors were putting it down to stress because of his situation and I had to fight to get any medical attention at all so he had a heart attack and nearly died. We'd moved to Peterborough and I didn't really make a lot of friends there but I did a job share and they were marvellous and helped me through this terrible time.

When Petra and her husband moved back to this part of the country, she took on some responsibility for her mother, although she found her deteriorating condition difficult to handle:

Then I came back here and walked into all the problems with my mother - that year before we moved here Tim lost his job, had trouble finding another job and my mother burnt her house down.

My sister didn't want anything to do with her towards the end at all - she really had to cut her off for her own survival. I was the only person in the end who she had. Everybody else had to abandon her simply for their own survival. When I lived away I could maintain that relationship from a distance but moving here she was only 9/10 miles away. She died fairly soon - by that time she'd got extremely bad cirrhosis of the liver and her second husband had left her and she had just gone downhill. She went into hospital from the burns from this fire she'd had and then she came out and of course she wanted me to look after her, but I just couldn't so she went into a nursing home -eventually discharged herself. She came out on the Friday and the snow came that Friday night and I thought at least she can't get out and get a drink - she was in a warden place, but she did get out and, I don't blame her really, she was dying, she knew she was dying but she drank ... and went back into hospital and her parting words to me 'I hope you rot in hell' because I wouldn't take her on. I couldn't. I might as well have gone and buried myself in the garden ...

I asked Petra why she had decided to return to education when she did and she told me she had done the occasional O-level when she was moving around the country, initially encouraged by a supportive colleague:

Maureen (a colleague) said, go and do Sociology - you'll enjoy it, and I thought I'd give it a try but I thought I would never pass, because I'd left school with no qualifications ... they had to show me how to write an essay because I didn't know and to my surprise I passed and I think it was that that triggered everything off ...

She also recognised that her job prospects would be enhanced with some academic qualifications:

Then I thought I'd do English because it needed improving and also I was looking at jobs in the civil service around that time and needed two O levels so I actually did my GCSE exam two days before his heart attack ...

But she also discovered intrinsic satisfaction in education:

The college wrote to me with the details about the access course and I thought I quite fancy this. So I was seriously thinking of doing this course for its own sake because I found that I liked studying and to do it for a year full time would be marvellous, but that had to get shelved when we moved here ... but then I started the access course here ...

Her confidence grew through her achievement on the access course:

I was very pleased to come into the A level Sociology and the A level English lit. I think if I hadn't done that and seen that I could work along side A level students I don't think I would have had the confidence to go into HE.

She went on to tell me about her ambivalent feelings when she started at university. However, her confidence has grown to the extent that she did not mention concerns about the work, but about her subsequent employment:

I didn't really think I would survive that first year and I'm still wondering whether social work is what I should be doing but I suppose I'm gaining more confidence as I'm going along ...

Petra's doubts over social work are clearly rooted in her experiences:

I think what bothers me with social work is that you don't qualify now as a generic social worker. You have what is called a focused area of practice which dominates your second year and I don't know what I want from my focused area - I don't really want to work with children and families. That's where the work is - that's where the jobs are but I don't think I could be objective ... Because of my ... I'd find it very distressing to leave the children in the situations that the law would say I have to leave them in.

I think this is a very significant comment. Petra told me she chose the social work course because she had done considerable part-time clerical work in social services and allied organisations. She seems to be looking for a professional qualification in an area concerned with people but at the same time is apprehensive of the personal challenges it will bring.

When the tape was switched off, over a cup of tea, she told me that her confidence had grown enormously since she had returned to full-time education. She also told me that she had enormous guilt feelings about her sister and mother.

As well as gaining her paper qualifications, Petra is benefiting from education through her growing confidence and being able to prove her ability. I think there are interesting links between her chosen course, her guilt feelings about her sister and mother and her ambivalence to social work as a career for her - links which, with hindsight, I wish I had pursued.

Working with disadvantaged groups, albeit in a different setting, is also Sheila's ultimate goal.

Sheila

Sheila is 40 and married with no children - her only child died a few years ago. She is in the third year of a four-year degree course with a social work qualification at a local university. Her story starts when she was quite young, at home, the youngest by eight years of five children. She is the only child of her mother, but has four half-brothers and sisters. She took the 11+ but her success was not the happy event she felt it should have been, though in hindsight she is more accepting of her parent's attitude:

> Sheila: I passed my Eleven Plus to go to the grammar school ... and then being told not to get my hopes up because I wouldn't be able to go to university. In actual fact I think it was quite a worry to them that I was even going to grammar school for financial reasons. It was quite a prestigious grammar school, very expensive uniform and equipment and I think that caused quite a worry to my father.

> Everybody else's parents seemed to be celebrating this thing. The other people in my class at school got bikes and watches and things and you also got your name in the paper - your parents have to take your name and a letter, and that didn't happen for me. I was extremely unhappy ... upset and angry. It's only looking back now that I also can see the worry that they had financially that I can handle all that you know. I don't think there were any sort of thoughts at all about me achieving, I think that generally speaking my parents just thought I'd get married and that it wasn't important.

Sheila felt that her education took second place to the domestic responsibilities which were expected of her as a young female. This appeared to cause considerable problems for her, particularly in school, but it reinforced the traditional gender role:

> I were very unhappy when I got to grammar school - lot of reasons, and one of them was that I always went to school with a sick feeling in my stomach when I hadn't done my homework and that were basically because at home I had jobs to do. My eldest sister by this time had just had her second child and was suffering post-natal depression ... and I used to have to go home and look after the children. I was the youngest female and I had to go and look after the children and put them to bed after school and I had things I had to do at home.

> I didn't say anything because ... right into finishing school I would have not had any sort of effect on my parents - my sister needed help with the children. But I was always getting into trouble. I'd manage to write something before the class started during break or dinner time. I have a very good memory of that and making up excuses. If I'd told the teachers what were happening then they would have to approach my parents and I'd be in trouble.

> I managed quite well in the third year and came out fourth in the whole class. Things were calmer at home and that allowed me to work.

The difference in the school/home ethos was not just in terms of attitude towards education; the hidden curriculum also affected Sheila. She felt isolated at the grammar school, unable to participate in extra-curricular activities and with no peer contact from her previous school. She left at the minimum leaving age:

> But there were other things as well, things like, I couldn't do what the others did, I didn't fit. I were probably, looking back, the poorest pupil in the year out of all the people I knew. Things like my blazer had a badge that was stitched on and my blazer had been somebody else's. It had wide lapels and this badge was different ...

> I left when I was fifteen, didn't take any exams ...

Sheila got a job with a chemist chain as a trainee dispensing assistant, but had to leave when she became pregnant at sixteen. The organisation not only operated a marriage bar, but also a policy of not employing visibly pregnant women:

You had to leave. To stay on after you got married you had to have special permission from the Area Manager and really it were only people who were well in ... It were 1969. I were pregnant and that actually ruled it out because you never, ever, ever had a pregnant woman behind the counter, so I couldn't even work there until I were, you know, later on in the pregnancy. I had to leave as I was getting married because, well I didn't have the permission to stay anyway, and being pregnant before I got married ...

Although she had only been working for a short period, her loss of financial independence was difficult for Sheila to handle:

I'd had quite a long period on this maternity allowance and I can remember when it had gone I was in a real panic that I didn't have any money at all. I hated it, I really hated it. There were no family allowance then, so I didn't have anything that was mine. Managing on one wage wasn't too bad because we never had much money anyway. It was my independence.

When I was pregnant I needed a coat because it was getting towards winter and I were big and none of my coats went round me and I can remember feeling totally humiliated, just asking. I suppose that, I thought that because the wage was actually paid for Joe's labour to him, it felt like his.

Like Jenny, she talks of fairness:

I weren't really aware of women's issues then and the only models that I had to go on were my parents. Mum didn't work and dad worked and you know he kept his wage. I didn't question that then but there was something, I couldn't explain where it came from, but something inside me somewhere along the line as a child I got this thing about fairness and I knew that I didn't have a fair share ... I don't know where that came from because I were bought up very much within the home to fulfil a women's role and yet there's something inside me about it's not fair.

After her son was born, Sheila gave up any thought of working until he was older. When he was five, he was diagnosed as having muscular dystrophy. During a fund-raising event at a local youth club, she was offered some part-time work, in the Youth Service, in the evenings. She talks of a mixture of feelings:

This job came up which was a life saver because finding out Neil had got Muscular Dystrophy I didn't think I'd ever be able to do anything. ... two conflicting feelings about first of all the grief that this were happening to Neil and I don't think I got the guilt thing, perhaps I did and I didn't acknowledge it ...

However, her evening work caused relationship problems between her and her husband, largely over the caring responsibility for their son, and she found it easier to enlist the help of others:

> It was usually two night a week, but it caused problems, not in the sense that we had arguments about it but purely and simply Neil was still my responsibility and so if it were Joe's shift week it were my responsibility to make arrangements for Neil. Even leisure - during the summer he played cricket and if he'd got a match on the night that I were at work it were my responsibility to find somebody. It was never Joe's responsibility but if he was there he would be quite happy about caring for Neil.

> When the training started, that involved some weekends and an extra night in the week. If I were on a training course at the weekend Neil would go and stay with my parents for the weekend and the extra night, if Joe were in he looked after him but I think probably because Neil liked to go to his grandparents so much, it was an easy way out rather than negotiate with Joe.

Around this time, Sheila 'went through a bad patch' of wanting to work full-time, which she felt was impossible because of her son. By this time, Neil was attending a school for physically disabled children, so she returned to college and did some O-levels. This was a day-time course, but she had set up a mutual support system with a neighbour whose child also went to the same school. However, by the time she started A-levels, her son, who was in his teens, needed a wheelchair and she had to leave college. She talked of this being a very painful time:

> It were a very emotional time for me ... it were a minefield of emotions.

> When Neil went into a wheelchair he put weight on very quickly and he was very soon in a position where my father couldn't lift him and so my father just couldn't carry him upstairs any more because of his weight. And that put an end to that support system as well. So, when Neil went into a wheelchair the support that I had very soon disappeared.

This period also created greater strain in her relationship. Sheila links this with the way her husband perceived their respective roles, but she also talks about control - her anger at her helplessness in the situation, and what her husband saw as her attempt to control him:

> Up to Neil's death I was always responsible, it were the biggest risk between Joe and myself. He would very often not come home in time and I'd have to make this judgement about, do I leave Neil with a drink watching TV or do I wait and if I went I would spend all evening thinking, worrying. If I didn't go, I'd be thinking about the kids waiting ... and I used to get really angry about it because I had all this pressure on me ... We didn't have a telephone then - I had to leave t'door open so that people could get in to him, the house were unsecure and it meant anybody could get in ... so he were left in a very vulnerable position.

> Sometimes you know there were anger and tears. There were pleading, everything, but we still couldn't agree. (I felt) completely utterly frustrated and even now Neil's been dead three years, it brings up all the anger that I felt then and it's one of those things that occurs when you're having a row about something.

These issues are clearly still fresh in her mind:

> ... my work didn't value. It's so unthinkable that Joe wouldn't be able to go to work in the morning because I wasn't there to look after Neil and yet that's what happened to me, I'd always be asking somebody to come and watch him, you know before Joe came home and it was, I can barely talk about it now, its ... We've talked about it and you know like these last two years and Joe will say it was about 'you can't tell me what to do ... ' He weren't exactly sitting at end of road in t'car to annoy me but he wouldn't stop work. But yea, it were about control.

When her son became really ill, Sheila gave up both studying and work to nurse him:

> When Neil fell really ill, I gave up work to nurse him. because by this time it could go literally from a sore throat in the morning to hospitalisation by evening - his health would deteriorate very quickly, and it were a case that if he were ill I wanted to be there because I could have lost him and I didn't want to be at work. It were my choice at that point - there were no questions about Joe giving work up because that's been the pattern all along.

From being quite young then, Sheila's identity has been largely defined, and certainly circumscribed by her gendered role, despite her resistance to it. Her son's death brought many emotions to the surface.

Apart from the obvious pain, she expressed a powerful loss of identity and fear of dependence. She was advised to take about a year before making any major decisions and this gave her time to think about her position:

> After he died I took some time out to sort myself out. it also meant that I were without a purpose. But it was - its strange really - the door had closed behind me and I'd this great vast something in front of me and it took some doing to step out into that.

> I was very aware very quickly that I were dependant on Joe for certain requirements. Up to that point I'd never ever been married simply for me, I was pregnant when I got married. I weren't aware of this through the marriage and yet as soon as I lost Neil I realised that we'd never just been alone really. I realised really quickly what a vulnerable position I was in, that if Joe decided that I didn't suit him any more, he certainly didn't need me for his child care requirements. Some friends of ours split up a few months before and that made me aware of my vulnerability and that's probably the reason why I questioned it so quickly. I realised that, that the few things I had left in the world were dependant upon Joe. I hated it so much I can't tell you. Had Joe left me at that point, I couldn't even see me, everything seemed to be gone or dependant upon Joe and I knew then that I had to do something very positive.

Sheila had thought about going to higher education some time before, and in fact had already begun A-levels, but again, it was her fear of dependence which was the major motivating factor:

> I'd known for a long time that one day Neil wouldn't be dependant upon me because we knew that he would die, probably late teens, which were when he did die. I knew that one day I wouldn't have any responsibilities and that I wanted to go to university ... it's been there quite a long time but I have to say I think that the things that actually drove me at the time after Neil's death were insecurity and fear ... it was panic of becoming dependent - very very strong fear.

> I'd made a decision not to go back to the Youth Service because I thought we'd both go to work in the day eventually and both come home ... it's not secure anyway ... After a year I were just about ready to start - we had a lot of marriage problems - he weren't handling his grief I know now and I were getting abusive phone calls every night. We had the phone number changed to ex-directory and they still kept coming. Neil's friend died a couple of months later. The day after the funeral I jumped out of bed, four o'clock in the morning ... and had a nervous breakdown. Another year passed - I had agoraphobia,

initially I'd been heavily sedated, when I came out of that, what I did were join some craft classes for a year to get back into it, then did the Access course.

During this period, Sheila was still dependent upon her husband 'which didn't help'. When I asked her what she had in mind when she chose the access course, her reply was a vehement 'independence!', but she also had a specific career aim: 'I knew I wanted to be a social worker'. Her desire for independence was so strong that although she had applied to the local universities she would have been prepared to move out of the area:

I applied for Austen University, the idea was that I would apply to Austen first. I wanted a degree and so the idea was that if I didn't get on (in Austen) I would then go anywhere in the country that would have me. I wanted to do Austen because of my parents and my marriage, but if Bath would have had me and Austen wouldn't I'd have gone to that.

She is in receipt of a grant but feels that her independence is violated because it is assessed on her husband's income and although he pays for her petrol and some books she still feels that it is a form of control:

My grant's assessed on Joe's income. I can't actually draw money out of my student account because there isn't enough. Joe pays for my petrol and my books, but I don't get what he should pay...

Her resentment extends beyond the financial situation between her and her husband, and she verbalises, like Jenny, the unfairness of the benefits system which in many instances appears to create dependency:

I don't think that it's fair that I'm not eligible for a full grant, but, I think what is really frustrating for me as well is being discriminated against because we actually have a marriage licence. There's those with long term partners - they're in a similar financial situation to me, they've never worked, you know 'cos they've had children but they haven't got a marriage licence, and they get a full grant.

Sheila's major benefit from education is her potential independence and an identity which is outside of her domestic role and over which she has some control. Her determination in this area is reflected in her response when I asked her whether she had had to negotiate with Joe about going to university:

No. I think that he knew in any case I was going - that there were no questions, I were going, and that it would have been a waste of time, had he not wanted me to go, to try and stop me because I would have gone.

Starting at university was one of the happiest days of my life ... I felt like I were always trying to get off, to go, and every time I got to the front door, something happened to stop me, and yet, all my life I think I knew I'd get there ...

I think mostly I'm just getting stronger and stronger, but I think the most important thing is that every day I'm there is another day closer - it just goes back to saying I want to be independent. I must say that independence is very strong, but also an identity is very very important. I need that identity and independence.

I asked Sheila whether she would move out of the immediate area for a job and whether she had discussed this with Joe:

That might shock him actually. In a way I've just taken it for granted that I would work somewhere within the area and I realised that I'm prepared to go anywhere to get a job. I don't mean leave Joe, but if I needed to go and work somewhere else for a couple of years to get experience and perhaps come back then I will. I haven't discussed it with him to be honest, not because I daren't speak to him about it or anything but only because it's been going through me head.

Again, the importance which Sheila attaches to independence comes through:

I must have given some thought to my marriage. I do actually want it to continue but I want it to continue because I want to be together, not because we're in any way dependent on each other. I've been thinking about this ... I'm forty one, I've been dependent all my adult life and if after all these years you can't stand it (separation for work) then perhaps we shouldn't be together, I'm not going to wait 'til I'm fifty five to regret, you know what's past. It'll be painful but if it happens it happens.

Her course is clearly making her examine her identity:

Recently you know, partly because of the course and all stuff we did like gender, I wonder what it were, what this seed were that was sown in my childhood, and if I could find it I'd go and give it to every other girl that I met ...

Sheila's return to education at all levels has clearly served many purposes - an identity outside the home, therapy, some control over her own life, the fulfilment of a long-held, though maybe not always verbalised, ambition, and a redress of the unfairness she perceives. Most importantly for her however, it is helping to meet her need for both financial and psychological independence.

Summary

This group of students experienced a variety of painful events which had a major effect on the course of their lives and defined their identities in particular ways at both private and public levels. The women's stories told of lives which had been closely circumscribed by powerful others and of a need to resist this control and gain some independence within their particular circumstances. For Gerry, the 'courage to do something' was central to the new self-image she was developing - 'the doing' seeming to be as important as the end product. Petra is gaining confidence and proving her ability through education. She also makes tentative links between her guilt feelings and her future career through the vehicle of education. Sheila, like Jenny in the previous chapter, talks about redress of the unfairness she has experienced because of her gendered identity. Her higher education course is the fulfilment of a long-held ambition which will give her financial and psychological independence.

Overall the students talked of confidence, a more positive self-image, the respect of others, proving ability and independence, all of which are concerned with the women's need to re-define at least a part of their identities in their own way through education. I have an impression of women fighting for personal survival, not in a physical, but in a psychological sense and education is the vehicle they are using. For all the women, education could be seen as therapeutic in its broadest sense.

8 Conclusion

The benefits for many women who return to learning, appear to be considerably more far-reaching than just the paper qualifications which education may bring. Before summarising and drawing some conclusions about what these benefits are, I want to present one woman's story in detail.

I have decided to present what Della told me separately from the others, not only because of its intensely painful nature and the powerful links with education, but also because of the almost accidental way in which it was collected. This reinforces not only the frequency of the link between education and the extent of trauma in women's lives, but also the importance of listening when collecting social data. If I had used only my own agenda when I talked to this woman, rather than being prepared to recognise hers, I may not have collected this very rich and interesting material and the exciting potential of the data could well have been overlooked.

During the course of my discussion with local college staff, it was suggested that in order to gain more background information on women's issues, I should talk to a particular voluntary worker whose post brought her into contact with many students. When I went along to see her, she did indeed confirm that students came to her with many problems and that there was a gender dimension to their difficulties, but what she went on to recount was an extremely traumatic personal history.

Della's story

Della is aged 40, divorced and has three children. She returned to education two years ago as a full-time student at a local college and has completed an access course. During the access course she applied for and succeeded in getting a voluntary part-time post with the Students' Union, based at the same college. She has taken a sabbatical and continued with that this year. Her elder daughter is in her second year at university, her younger daughter is at the same college as Della. Her son, aged 13 is at a school in the area which provides for special educational needs.

She was second oldest in a working class (her categorisation) family of seven children and her traumatic experiences started early, though she may not have recognised them as such at the time:

> My mother was always putting us down. There were seven of us, the oldest was my sister, she (her mother) always said to us that she never wanted any of us except her, you know, blatantly, in the face 'I never wanted any of you' and I think when I got to the age of 10 I started rebelling against her for putting all her crap on me and I hated her, I still do - I was worthless and never wanted ...

Her rebellion was reflected in her refusal to go to grammar school, to do homework, to wear school uniform and to do the traditional 'female subjects' such as cookery and needlework. She seemed to constantly challenge school authority:

> I eventually got expelled in my fourth year ... I wouldn't conform to their views of what girls should be, so I was out. They would say 'you will do this' and I would say 'but what for, why?' and I would flatly refuse to do homework. I would question what the teachers said. Everybody else sat there 'she's going to be in trouble again'. I thought 'well it's not trouble, I want to know why' and it eventually came to one teacher, I had been off about two weeks with tonsillitis and I came back and they said 'have you done your homework?' and I said 'no, I didn't know anything about it in the first place' so , you know the tubes they put papers in? Well, he hit me with one of them and I hit him back and that was it you know - out you go - so I went and got a job - 15 and a bit.

Della had a good relationship with her father though:

> My father was totally different, he was always there. He stood by us regardless. If there was trouble or anything else he was there, but he died the day before I got married. He died on the Friday and I got married on the Saturday ...

She married at 19 and had her first child at 20:

> I think my life just ended, I got stuck in the usual role of me being at home with a child, no help, no support and just sort of festering ...

> I was screaming inside, I was dying. I thought well, I will become this mother. I accepted I've got this child and I've got this husband that didn't work but can always find money to go out drinking. He never helped in any way and I didn't get help from my mother. Basically, I cut her off. My sister and my two older brothers, they've

got their own families. My husband's side were a typical working class family and they kept themselves to themselves, they helped each other but wouldn't help me - because I wasn't born of their name and I was somebody else's daughter.

Over the next six years she had two more children, by which time she was 26. The violence started after her third child was born.

He was domineering. What he said went. I'd fallen in the trap - very dependent. Before the last child was born there was no signs of physical violence and then when Jon was born in 1980 the physical violence started. I was trying to question - what have I done? I'd find something I'd done to justify what he done to me - I didn't do this right or I said that wrong or his tea wasn't ready, silly stupid things. The violence got worse. You know - the push became a hit and the hit became a punch and the punches became harder and then I've had my legs broken, I've had black eyes, I've had my teeth knocked out, my lips split, fingers broken and when he knocked my front teeth out, Jon would be three, the eldest ten and the other one seven. He left that night, he actually came back about three hours later, said he'd been to his sister's and called up and couldn't get any answer ... He said he'd reported himself, I thought 'hah, yes of course he had'. Now every time I got an injury I told the hospital or the doctor that he'd done it but I told him that I had made an excuse.

About a week after he had knocked my teeth out he came in the house and I thought 'you'd do worse if you don't let him back in'. I got all the threats as usual and I said 'if your hand comes near me again I'll stab you'. The violence stopped for about two or three months and then he got back into his old routine. He came at me and I got a knife and I threatened him. From that he didn't physically hurt me and the violence was, I could see it coming, the violence was directed at my eldest daughter. All this time his family knew what he was doing, I never told any of mine - I thought 'it's my problem and I'll sort it out' but his family knew and I couldn't understand why they had never said anything to him - come to see me or anything else and that's when I thought 'it's because I'm somebody else's daughter'. Their daughters had had violence from their partners and the whole family had charged up and sorted them out but I thought 'they haven't done it for me. Where are they?' His mother actually turned round and said 'well he's your husband after all and you have to accept what comes', and I said 'no I don't'. I'd been through enough they (the children) hadn't actually been physically hurt by then but I knew they were mentally and emotionally hurting.

It came to this particular night and Donna would be 14½ getting ready for her mock exams Jon was quite small and talks a lot and she was getting on with revising and all she said was 'Jon would you mind keeping quiet while I'm revising?' Well, he blew his top. He went nuts - he threatened to put her through a window. He went into t'kitchen, he got a hammer, he smashed every stick of furniture in the house, every single bit. Jon and Katie the middle daughter they went upstairs. I thought 'they'll just be holding each other'. I was scared Donna was going to get it obviously ... and I was scared that if I joined in I was going to get it as well ... This went on for two or three hours at least. All this screaming and shouting going on. He hadn't hit her yet but I could see it coming so I grabbed Donna and said to go over the road to her friend Denise and stay there. I said 'I'll sort it out' and one almighty fight and that's the time I ended up with broken fingers and a split lip and where I got strength from I don't know but I threw him out. I locked the doors, threw all his clothes out, straight out of the bedroom window, called the police. They came and it was, well it's done with, it's a domestic and you know a typical male attitude, they couldn't see what we had been through and they were going to let him get away with it again.

The next morning Donna phoned and I said 'you can come home now he's not coming back again'. She said 'but you said that before'. 'I know I said it before but this time this is it'. 'But you've said that before', and I said 'I know, you're going to have to trust me on this one, we've all had enough'. That was on the Friday night. On the Monday morning I went straight round to the solicitor's. I got a solicitor - a nice woman and I gave everything to her, the whole lot. After a while she began issuing divorce proceedings. The papers were delivered to him by private detective and three months later another set of papers were delivered and still no response and then it was like nine or ten months and still no response. He said he hadn't received them and we had to appeal to the court to say 'look, he has received these papers three times', and they had to take a statement from the private detective who said 'yes, the papers containing this, this and this, I have delivered three times and there has been no response' and it went through. Well, it started to go through and he wanted access to Jon, not the girls they weren't his he always said, none of them were his but he wanted access to Jon basically because he is the only son and he is the only one to carry that family name on. ... I didn't want Jon to see him, then I thought if I just said no he's going to make trouble, so I did it on a voluntary basis. Saturday I was to drop him off about 11 and pick him up about 4, and I used to dread picking him up. In the few minutes I dropped Jon off and the few minutes when I picked him up I got 'I want to kill you, you're going to die' ... He used to phone up, passing all these threats down the phone all through the night. I told my solicitor this and she said 'what you have to do now is every time he says something when you see him or on t'phone write the date and time down'. I did and I had this huge pile of papers. Donna continued to work for her GCSE's. She got nine all A's and B's - how, I'll never know.

It came to the family court because he was contesting custody ... They said I was how did they say, mentally disturbed. I used to believe this - I was going mental.

And he wanted Jon so desperately he couldn't be bothered to turn up at the family court for the custody hearing so custody went to me anyway. I couldn't see it going any other way and he continued to see his dad but it got to the stage where I couldn't take him, someone else used to take him. Then on a Friday after about a year or so Jon refused to go. He screamed abuse at me. He'd come back on a Saturday in tears, screaming at me in temper. I thought he must be doing something to him or the family must be saying something. Well I took him to the doctor's and said 'well look, this is what's happening - he's constantly wetting t'bed, constantly screaming and shouting in his sleep'. He referred him to t'child psychiatrist at the children's hospital and on the first session there were tears and the only thing he could say was he didn't want to turn out like his dad.

I sit with Jon as well - even to this day he'll not go in by himself. The psychiatrist found out that he (his father) had been saying all these things to him - what he's going to do to me, what he's going to do to Donna, what he's going to do to Katie and he'd kept it all to himself - he was 8 or 9.

Yes, besides these emotional mental problems he's got, he's got educational problems as well, quite bad ones. Whether this is due to what happened to him - he now attends a special needs school, for about 15 months now. He knows that nothing is anyone's fault now because he used to blame Donna and she believed it and she went into deep depression and she couldn't go to the doctors. I went to the doctor's and explained it to him ... How I've managed to cope with all the crap, with Jon's problems and Donna's depression, I don't know how I managed to bring her out of that ...

Following the divorce. Della's two younger children had quite severe emotional problems which she is still helping them resolve. She spent the first year after her divorce helping them through the trauma, although she recognised a need in herself to 'do something - I wanted something for me'. The following year she was persuaded by her elder daughter to enrol in the local college:

> She said 'Why don't you go to college?' 'No I can't do that, it's only for young people'. I'd been out of education you know 24 years and I just said no, I really wanted to go but I was too scared, absolutely terrified – 'what is this older woman going to do in college with all these young people?' I didn't want to but she bullied and bullied me until I actually came down and I ended up doing 3 GCSEs.

> She said I could do it, but I didn't think I could, for about the first six months I was packing it in every week ... it was just having that motivation, a bit more get up and go, confidence ...

Despite having a great deal of stress-related illness, she enrolled the following year, after some persuasion, on the Access course which she completed with ease. This gave her a great deal of pride in her achievement:

> I got some confidence back then and I started the second year on access. Everybody was in this access room - who are you, have you got any previous qualifications, and there were no qualifications, no qualifications and I'd got qualifications and it went round and I thought nobody else had got anything! As you get to know one another during the first six or eight weeks the comments I got was 'when we went round that room and said who we were and what we got, you looked so confident, really voiced out'. I thought 'Oh great!'.

> It got to about February as we started in the September and I got all the credits done easy ... I thought, 'God I've done it again!' I was so bloody proud of myself ... I got so many students coming up asking for help ...

Della's confidence had grown greatly during this period, so much so that she was persuaded to take on a voluntary post within the college:

> So there was a vacancy for a voluntary post and a female lecturer said 'why don't you go for it?' and I thought 'no I can't do that', 'well you can always give it a try'. So I did and that was my first involvement with it. I thought it was absolutely wonderful, it gave me even more confidence.

As well as boosting her confidence, it has also given her some power over defining her identity. It is not a new or different identity, but an aspect of her which she is developing. She has respect and prestige in this job which makes her feel that she is a worthwhile person:

> Now I'm President of the whole college, I was elected by ballot. I love what I do now if it could be a permanent job, but I know it's not. I've helped a lot of female students a hell of a lot. When its induction week I go round to classes and at the end I always say 'if you have problems whether its personal or academic don't just sit there you get up and tell someone and if they don't listen you come to me and I will try and sort it out for you'. It gives me great satisfaction and pleasure that I help someone whose been down and not known how to get out of it. I love been around students young and old, it doesn't make any different to me what they are who they are ...

> I have got all my confidence back and great satisfaction with my work. I'm going to do the next academic year then I'll go on to do a B.Ed.

This confidence has spilled over into other areas of her life. Her son was still having severe psychological problems as a result of the trauma and had been excluded from school. She took on the might of the local education authority, refusing to accept that it could be up to two years before he could be placed in a school which was equipped to help him with his difficulties:

> I didn't have a clue how to do it but since I got that confidence back I thought 'I can do that and I can do this and my child is not going to do without an education for 18 months to two years till they decide to find him a place'. ... So I found him a school ... Education said 'you can't do this', and I said, 'yes I can ... I can do anything I like ...' I started Jon in a special school before they actually started their paperwork.

Della's return to education has been a major factor in her returning confidence. It is however a somewhat tenuous confidence, which was illustrated when I asked her what plans she had:

> I'm going to do this year, I don't feel, I'm not quite ... probably because of my emotions ... doing what I do now and doing what I did last year I feel safe ... I'm going to stand again next year then I will go on ... I want to do a B.Ed in special needs ... Now I'm scared of nothing, but sometimes I am ... I don't know, ... in HE there's not going to be that personal support like I've had here ... I'm not ready,

until I've dealt with everything I need to deal with within me then I don't think I can go ...

Della's experiences have clearly been very painful, both physically and psychologically and she is searching for a positive, acceptable self-image. Her daughter has played a key role in persuading Della that she could do it, which she acknowledges, but at the same time, she is determined to be independent:

> The original goal was not my goal, it was Donna's goal - I will go on to higher education, and I thought 'if I can do this, I can do that quite easily' and then we still had these mega problems with John ... I was being pressurised by Donna and by the college. I said 'yes, I'm going to do it', then I thought, 'no, I'm not, I'm going to do it in my own time, when I'm ready'.

This determination was reflected in her closing comment:

> There are still barriers I keep up where people are not allowed in, no one in. In here is me, myself and I and there are parts of me that nobody else can have, not even the kids, they belong to me.

Della makes all the links with education which other students make, and is aware of the role of education as a vehicle for change, in only in her own life, but also in that of others. Her final comment emphasises the need for her be her own person, at least in part, and she is actively working to exert some power and control over her life. This is true not only for Della of course, it is threaded right through the stories of all the students I interviewed.

What is in education for women?

Throughout all of my talks with the students, I was struck by their courage and determination to change aspects of their lives, often in the face of considerable resistance and difficulties. Women return to education for many reasons and it is very clear that those I spoke with were gaining a great deal more from their return to education than just paper qualifications. The following few extracts epitomise the many links which were made:

> It's made me value me a lot I think, it's made me see myself a lot differently, and I'm a lot happier about myself.

> I had actually achieved something ... in the scheme of things it wasn't very much but to me it was a lot.

> I'm proud of myself, to be honest, I'm very proud of myself ...

It boosts your confidence and it all makes you feel much better.

I've got more confidence now than what I've ever had really.

Definitely something personal. I wanted to prove to people that I had got some worth. It's given me something positive.

The main issue? I think getting rid of little skeletons in the cupboard ... the course has helped. I wouldn't have done it without being on the course.

You've got a life out of home haven't you?

I might not get chance to do much with it but at least I know I've achieved something.

Starting at university was one of the happiest days of my life ...

Independence is very strong, but also an identity is very very important. I need that identity and independence.

These extracts are a reflection of the changing and more positive perceptions which the women have of themselves. Changes such as increasing confidence, fulfilment, a more positive self-image, independence and so on are over-arching themes, threaded through all the narratives, but are perhaps more powerfully evident in those which included painful experiences.

The links between identity and education were made in a variety of ways, none of which was mutually exclusive. For some students, such as Denise, it was proof of ability, for others, like Nola, this was perhaps associated with a better job. Sometimes, as with Jenny, it was simply associated with the status which education was perceived as bringing with it.

Those women who were partnered with domestic responsibilities often made links between education and their domestic identity. This sometimes took the form of outright resentment and resistance to it, as with Colette. In other instances it was a desire for an identity outside of the home, as well as being a housewife, wife or mother which was important. As Frances told me:

... it's something to be proud of - something for yourself and not for them. You've got a life out of home.

For a large number, particularly those who talked of painful experiences, education is linked with a desire to remedy a negative self-image influenced by the attitude and behaviour of significant others, and a way of shedding stigma associated with the past. Often, this negative self-image was imposed (and sometimes resisted) from a very early age, and education seems to be a means by which many of the students were taking back some power and control over the way in which their identity had been defined. Alison, for example, talked about her feelings of shame at being a teenage unmarried mother - feelings which persist fifteen years after the birth of her daughter. She spoke of a poor self-image and a need to prove to people 'that I had got some worth'. Gerry talked about the stigma of the sexual abuse she experienced in her childhood, despite the fact that none of her family or friends knows about it. She went on to speak of proving to others that she has some ability and is a worthwhile person. For Della of course, her need to define her own identity was manifest in both her educational achievement and in her obvious pride in the voluntary post she has – 'elected by the whole college'.

The women also talked of the development of a part of their identity which had been latent. For many of them, the 'real me' was emerging - this was particularly evident with Dilys and Sheila for example, both of whom had felt that someday they would return to learning and compensate for what they had been denied in their youth. Quite often with her increasing confidence, a student's perception of herself changed whilst she was in education and it was almost as if she was discovering a different self - Vida puts this nicely:

> I think gradually it has been a metamorphosis of me.

For most of the women, education was linked with a need for some independence, which was not necessarily financial. Regardless of the social or economic position of the student, or her course, this was associated with resistance to the power and control that others have or have had over her identity, in the public and private spheres of her life. Thus, whether this was directly or indirectly verbalised, education can be associated with the desire by many of the women to take charge of at least a part of the content and direction of their own lives. For some of the students, this was a small part of the whole, operating within their existing circumstances. For others, it represented a major life change, either potential or actual.

There is evidence that the identities of the students I talked to have been controlled and constrained by the overlapping and interlocking nature of the dominant patriarchal ideology in our society. The women are not totally enmeshed by this control however, and there are ample indications of their resistance to it, through the vehicle of education. It is not necessarily that the women are looking for a new identity, rather it seems to be an edited version of an identity over which they feel they have had insufficient control. All the students have acted in their own interests and shown considerable autonomy and agency. All of them have shown tremendous courage and resolve in realising their desire. Jenny, for example, is determined to carve out a different sort of identity for herself, despite physical and psychological pressure not only from her husband, but also from her neighbourhood. Gerry is determined to overcome the controlling effects of her sexual abuse. Deidre and Grace are resisting the ongoing power of their ex-husbands. Leila and Petra are working to change the effects of many negative impacts on their identities. All of them are using education as a vehicle for their own reasons and one could argue that the choice the women made to return to education is in itself indicative of this. It seems difficult to deny though that the research findings reveal that this agency is still framed within an overall patriarchal social structure. This is evidenced throughout, and particularly in Colette's ambivalence about her feelings and possible future action.

Thus, the return to education can be seen as a clear attempt by women to change at least some aspect of their lives. The gains which the students were talking about, apart from the obvious paper qualifications, were fulfilment, an increasing confidence, a positive self-image and independence, all of which I have put under the umbrella term of identity. One or two students in fact did mention a 'different' identity. If we look at the converse of these gains - low confidence, lack of fulfilment, dependence and poor self-image and link them back into the women's stories, it can be argued that the patriarchal structure of society was instrumental either directly, or indirectly, in influencing these negative aspects of the students' identity. The women's return to education, taking some control over their own lives and acting in their own interests, has effected some change.

Although there is no published research that I know of which links traumatic experiences with education, discussion of my research with colleagues in a variety of professional settings has provided anecdotal support for the findings. Even so, I would not have expected around half of the students to present these kinds of experiences, but it did raise the question for me of whether there is this frequency in the population generally, or whether women with this type of experience are attracted to education for a particular reason.

People generally do not have just one reason for doing things and it may well be that trauma is not the sole motivating factor, but may be a contributing factor. Is the women's return a multi-step situation, for example, early school leaving, *plus* an unfulfilling job, *plus* trauma, *plus* a possible relationship problem, *plus* a number of other unknown factors in any order or combination?

One could also raise the issue of whether education is *the* major vehicle or one of many which women who have experienced trauma in their lives use to take control over some aspects of their identity. Implicit in what the students have said is the status which education brings but there may well be other vehicles such as a craft or music or starting a business which women choose for their purpose as well as education.

It could perhaps be argued that the findings in themselves are highly speculative since the research was conducted in and around one northern city, by a single feminist researcher. I have also asked myself the question of whether I had somehow got a special group, despite the care taken at the interview stage. However, the students did come from a wide range of demographic and socio-economic backgrounds, and the common themes, which I have used in the analysis, are grounded in the data.

Nevertheless, my research sample was small and the results of the research, whatever their impact, cannot be extrapolated to a wider population. What they have done though is provide a basis for further, rigorous wide-scale research of both a qualitative and quantitative nature, in different geographical areas, to discover whether this research is a single phenomenon due to a freak of sampling or whether it is an accurate reflection of women returners generally. This would address many of the questions and issues which I have raised.

What has emerged, uniquely, from this small and specific piece of research, is that the women in the study gained much more from their return to education than would at first seem to be the case.

The existence of trauma in people's lives is not necessarily exceptional in the lives of either women or men, and the older one is, the more likely there are to be painful experiences. What is certain though is that a high proportion of this particular group of mature women students presented, unexpectedly and unsolicited, painful life experiences, and there appear to be clear links between these experiences and their return to education. All of the women I spoke to talked of positive changes in the way they saw themselves since they had become students. I would like to think that their stories will encourage and support not only those of us who did return to education, but also those women who may tentatively be considering returning to a formal learning environment.

Bibliography

ACACE (1982), *Continuing Education: from Politics to Practice*, ACACE, Leicester.

Arnot, M. and Weiner, G. (1987), *Gender and the Politics of Schooling*, Open University Press and Hutchinson, London.

Barrett, M. (1980), *Women's Oppression To-day*, Verso, London.

Bell, J., Hamilton, S. and Roderick, G. (1986), *Mature Students: Entry to Higher Education. A Guide to Students and Advisers*, Longman, London.

Berger, P. and Luckman, T. (1991), *The Social Construction of Reality*, Penguin, Harmondsworth.

Boston, S. (1980), *Women Workers and the Trades Unions*, Davis Poynter, London.

Brannen, J. and Moss, P. (1988), *New Mothers at Work: Employment and Childcare*, Unwin Hyman, London.

Brittan, A. and Maynard, M. (1984), *Sexism, Racism and Oppression*, Blackwell, Oxford.

Browning, D. (1990), 'Beyond GCSE: Real Choices for Adults', *Adults Learning*, vol. 1(3), pp. 147-148.

Burchell, H. and Millman, V. (1989), *Changing Perspectives on Gender*, Open University Press, Milton Keynes.

Burr, V. (1998), *Gender and Social Psychology*, Routledge, London.

Butler, J. (1990), *Gender Trouble: feminism and the subversion of identity*, Routledge, London.

Cameron, D. (1992), *Feminism and Linguistic Theory (second edition)*, Macmillan, Basingstoke.

Cameron, D. (ed) (1998), *The Feminist Critique of Language (second edition)*, Routledge, London.

Central Statistical Office (1999), *Social Trends*, HMSO, London.

Charles, N. (1993), *Gender Divisions and Social Change*, Harvester Wheatsheaf, Hemel Hempstead.

Charnley, A.H., McGivney, V. and Sims, D. (1985), *Education for the Adult Unemployed: some responses*, NIACE, Leicester.

Coats, M. (1989), 'Support for Women Learners: Requirements and Resources', *Adults Learning*, vol. 1(4), pp. 104-105.

Coats, M. (1994), *Women's Education*, SHRE and Open University Press, Buckingham.

Connell, R.W. (1987), *Gender and Power*, Polity, Cambridge.

Connell, R.W. (1995), *Masculinities*, University of California Press, Berkeley.

Cooley, C.H. (1962), *Social Organisation: A Study of the Larger Mind*, Schocken, New York.

Cooley, C.H. (1964), *Human Nature and the Social Order*, University of Chicago Press, Chicago.

Daly, M. (1978), *Gyn/Ecology: The Metaethics of Radical Feminism*, Women's Press, London.

Daly, M. (1986), *Beyond God the Father: Towards a Philosophy of Women's Liberation*, Women's Press, London.

Damon, W. and Hart, D. (1988), *Self-understanding in Childhood and Adolescence*, Cambridge University Press, Cambridge.

Dawkins, R. (1976), *The Selfish Gene*, Oxford University Press, New York.

De Beauvoir, S. (1972), *The Second Sex*, Penguin, Harmondsworth.

Deem, R. (1980), *Schooling for Women's Work*, Routledge and Kegan Paul, London.

Delamont, S. (1990), *Sex Roles and the School*, Routledge, London.

Delphy, C. (1984), *Close to Home: A Materialist Analysis of Women's Oppression*, Hutchinson, London.

Delphy, C. (1993), 'Rethinking Sex and Gender', *Women's Studies International Forum*, vol. 16(1), pp. 1-9.

Delphy, C. and Leonard, D. (1992), *Familiar Exploitation*, Polity, Cambridge.

Dennis, N., Henriques, F. and Slaughter, C. (1956), *Coal is Our Life*, Eyre and Spottiswood, London.

Draper, J. (1993), 'We're back with Gobbo: The Re-establishment of Gender Relations following a School Merger', in P. Woods and M. Hammersley (eds), *Gender and Ethnicity in Schools: Ethnographic Accounts*, Routledge, London.

Dworkin, A. (1981), *Pornography: Men Possessing Women*, The Women's Press, London.

Edwards, R. (1993), *Mature Women Students*, Taylor and Francis, London.

Eysenck, H.J. (1967), *The Biological Basis of Personality*, Charles C. Thomas, Springfield, Illinois.

Firestone, S. (1979), *The Dialectic of Sex: the Case for Feminist Revolution*, The Women's Press, London.

Foucault, M. (1981), *The History of Sexuality Volume 1: Introduction*, Penguin, Harmondsworth.

Franks, S. (1999), *Having None of It*, Granta, London.

Further Education Unit (1991), *Support and Guidance Needs of Adult Students: Final Report*, FEU, Yorkshire and Humberside Regional Office, Dewsbury.

Glaser, B. and Strauss A. (1967), *The Discovery of Grounded Theory: Strategies for Qualitative Research*, Aldine, Chicago.

Goffman, E. (1968), *Stigma*, Pelican, Harmondsworth.

Goldberg, S. (1979), *Male Dominance: The Inevitability of Patriarchy*, Abacus Sphere Books, London.

Greer, G. (1999), *The Whole Woman*, Doubleday, London.

Hakim, C. (1979), *Occupational Segregation: A Comparative Study of the Degree and Pattern of the Differentiation between Men and Women's Work in Britain, U.S. and Other Countries*, Department of Employment Research Paper No. 9, HMSO, London.

Hanmer, J. and Saunders, S. (1984), *Well-founded Fear*, Hutchinson, London.

Hubbard, R. (1983), 'Social Effects of Some Contemporary Myths about Women', in M. Lowe and R. Hubbard (eds), *Women's Nature*, Pergamon, Oxford.

Hughes, M., Kennedy, M., MacCaffery, J. and McGivney, V. (1989), 'Editorial', *Adults Learning*, vol. 1(4), p. 99.

Jackson, S. (1978), 'The Social Context of Rape: Sexual Scripts and Motivation', *Women's Studies International Quarterly*, vol. 1, pp. 27-38.

Jenkins, R. (1996), *Social Identity*, Routledge, London.

Kelly, L. (1988), *Surviving Sexual Violence*, Polity, Cambridge.

Land, H. (1985), 'The Introduction of Family Allowances: an Act of Historic Justice?', in C. Ungerson (ed), *Women and Social Policy*, Macmillan, Basingstoke.

Lees, S. (1986), *Losing Out: Sexuality and Adolescent Girls*, Hutchinson, London.

Lees, S. (1994), *Getting Away with Date Rape: Rape Masquerading as Seduction*, Conference Paper, British Sociology Association, University of Central Lancashire, Preston.

Lees, S. (1997), *Ruling Passion: Sexual Violence, Reputation and the Law*, Open University Press, Buckingham.

Lewis, J. (1991), *Women in Britain: Women, the Family, Work and the State, since 1945*, Blackwell, Oxford.

London Rape Crisis Centre (1984), *Sexual Violence: the Reality for Women*, Women's Press, London.

Lucas, S. and Ward, P. (1985), 'Mature Students at Lancaster University', *Adult Education*, vol. 58(2), pp. 151-157.

MacKinnon, C. (1982), 'Feminism, Marxism, Method and the State: An Agenda for theory', *Signs*, vol. 7(3), pp. 515-544.

Maclean, M. and Groves, D. (eds) (1991), *Women's Issues in Social Policy*, Routledge, London.

Marshment, M. (1997), 'The Picture is Political: Representation of Women in Contemporary Popular Culture', in V. Robinson and D. Richardson (eds), *Introducing Women's Studies (second edition)*, Macmillan, Basingstoke.

McGivney, V. (1993), *Women, Education and Training: Barriers to Access, Informal Starting Points and Progression Routes*, NIACE, Leicester.

Mead, R. (1934), *Mind, Self and Society from the Standpoint of a Social Behaviourist*, University of Chicago Press, Chicago.

Miles, M.B. and Huberman, A.M. (1994), *Qualitative Data analysis (second edition)*, Sage, London.

Millett, K. (1970), *Sexual Politics*, Virago, London.

Moir, A. and Jessel, D. (1989), *BrainSex: The Real Difference Between Men and Women*, Michael Joseph, London.

Mooney, J. (1993), *The Hidden Figure: Domestic Violence in North London*, Research Paper, Centre for Criminology, Middlesex University, Middlesex.

Nash, T. (1990), 'The Great No-Win Situation', *Director*, vol. 43(4), pp. 46-50.

Newell, S. (1993), 'The Superwoman Syndrome: Gender Differences in Attitudes towards Equal Opportunities at Work and towards Domestic Responsibilities at Home', *Work, Employment and Society*, vol. 7(2), pp. 275-289.

Nussbaum, M. (1996), 'The Sleep of Reason ... is a Female Nightmare', *Times Higher Education Supplement*, 2 February, p. 17, Times Newspapers, London.

Oakley, A. (1993), *Sex, Gender and Society (revised edition)*, Arena/New Society, Aldershot.

Parr, J. (1991), *The Experience of Mature Women Students in Further and Higher Education*, M.Ed Thesis, The University of Sheffield.

Parr, J. (1996), *Education: What's in it for Mature Women?*, PhD Thesis, The University of Sheffield.

Pascall, G. and Cox, R. (1993), *Women Returning to Higher Education*, SHRE and Open University Press, Milton Keynes.

Pillinger, J. (1992), *Feminising the Market: Women's Pay and Employment in the European Community*, Macmillan, Basingstoke.

Poster, M. (1978), *Critical Theory of the Family*, Pluto Press, London.

Pye, J. (1991), *Second Chances: Adults Returning to Education*, Oxford University Press, Oxford.

Reissman, C.K. (1987), 'When Gender is not enough: Women Interviewing Women', *Gender and Society*, vol. 1(2), pp. 172-207.

Reskin, B. and Padavic, I. (1994), *Women and Men at Work*, Pine Forge Press, London.

Rich, A. (1977), *Of Women Born: Motherhood as Experience and Institution*, Virago, London.

Rich, A. (1980), 'Compulsory Heterosexuality and Lesbian Experience', *Signs*, vol. 5(4), pp. 631-660.

Richardson, D. (1997), 'Sexuality and Male Dominance' in V. Robinson and D. Richardson (eds), *Introducing Women's Studies (second edition)*, Macmillan, Basingstoke.

Robson, C. (1993), *Real World Research*, Blackwell, Oxford.

Rose, H, (1985), 'Women's Refuges: Creating New Forms of Welfare?', in C. Ungerson (ed), *Women and Social Policy*, Macmillan, Basingstoke.

Russell, D. (1984), *Sexual Exploitation: Rape, Child Sexual Abuse and Workplace Harassment*, Sage, London.

Sayers, J. (1982), *Biological Politics*, Tavistock, London.

Schutze, H.G. (ed), Slowey, M., Wagner, A. and Paquet, P. (1987), *Adults in Higher Education: Policies and Practice in Great Britain and North America*, Almqvist and Wiksell International, Stockholm.

Scott, J. (1991), *Who Rules Britain?*, Polity, Cambridge.

Seidler, V. J. (1994), *Recovering the Self: Morality and Social Theory*, Routledge, London.

Serbin, L.A. (1984), 'Teachers, Peers and Play Preferences', in S. Delamont (ed), *Readings on Interaction in the Classroom*, Methuen, London.

Sharpe, S. (1994), *Just Like a Girl (second edition)*, Penguin, Harmondsworth.

Sieber, J. (1992), *Planning Ethically Responsible Research*, Applied Social Research Methods Series Vol. 31, Sage, London.

Skelton, C. (1997), 'Women and Education' in V. Robinson and D. Richardson (eds), *Introducing Women's Studies (second edition)*, Macmillan, Basingstoke.

Smith, D. (1988), *The Everyday World as Problematic: A Feminist Sociology*, Open University Press, Milton Keynes.

Spender, D. (1980), *Man Made Language*, Routledge, London.

Spender, D. (1983), *Women of Ideas: and what Men have done to Them...*, Ark Paperbacks, London.

Spender, D. and Sarah, E. (eds) (1988), *Learning to Lose: Sexism in Education (second edition)*, Women's Press, London.

Stacey, J. (1997), 'Untangling Feminist theory', in V. Robinson and D. Richardson (eds), *Introducing Women's Studies (second edition)*, Macmillan, Basingstoke.

Stanworth, M. (1983), *Gender and Schooling*, Hutchinson, London.

Stevens, R. (1994), 'Evolutionary Origins of Identity' in J. Anderson and M. Ricci (eds), *Society and Social Science: A Reader (second edition)*, The Open University, Milton Keynes.

Strauss, A. and Corbin, J. (1990), *Basics of Qualitative Research: Grounded Theory, Procedures and Techniques*, Sage, London.

Taylor, S. and Bogdan, R. (1984), *Introduction to qualitative research methods*, John Wiley, Chichester.

Thorne, B. (1993), *Gender Play: Girls and Boys in School*, Open University Press, Buckingham.

Wakeford, N. (1993), 'Beyond Educating Rita: Mature Students and Access Courses', *Oxford Review of Education*, vol. 19(2).

Walby, S. (1986), *Patriarchy at Work*, Polity, Cambridge.

Walby, S. (1989), 'Theorizing Patriarchy', *Sociology*, vol. 23(2), pp. 213-234.

Walby, S. (1990), *Theorizing Patriarchy*, Blackwell, Oxford.

Walby, S. (1997), *Gender Transformations*, Routledge, London.

Walter, N. (1999), *The New Feminism*, Virago, London.

Warde, A. and Hetherington, K. (1993), 'A changing domestic division of labour? Issues of measurement and interpretation', *Work, Employment and Society*, vol. 7(1), pp. 23-45.

Weeks, J. (1990), *Sex, Politics and Society*, Longman, London.

Williams, F. (1989), *Social Policy: A Critical Introduction*, Polity, Cambridge.

Wilson, E. (1977), *Women and the Welfare State*, Tavistock, London.

Wilson, E. (1983), 'Feminism and social policy', in M. Loney, D. Boswell and J. Clarke (eds), *Social Policy and Social Welfare*, Open University Press, Milton Keynes.

Woodley, A., Wagner, L., Slowey, M., Hamilton, M. and Fulton, O. (eds) (1987), *Choosing to Learn: Adults in Education*, SHRE and Open University Press, Milton Keynes.

Index